D0614583

JOURNALING

A Spirit Journey

JOURNALING

A Spirit Journey

———————————

Anne Broyles

THE UPPER ROOM

Nashville, Tennessee

JOURNALING: A SPIRIT JOURNEY

Copyright © 1988 Anne Broyles. All rights reserved.

No part of this book may be reproduced in any manner whatso-ever without written permission of the publisher except in brief quotations embodied in critical articles or reviews. For informa-tion, address The Upper Room, 1908 Grand Avenue, P.O. Box 189, Nashville, Tennessee 37202.

Scripture quotations not otherwise identified are from the Revised Standard Version of the Bible, copyrighted 1946, 1952, and © 1971 by the Division of Christian Education, National Council of Churches of Christ in the United States of America, and are used by permission.

Scripture quotations designated TEV are from the *Good News Bible, The Bible in Today's English Version*, copyright by American Bible Society 1966, 1971, © 1976, and are used by permission.

Scripture quotations designated NEB are from *The New English Bible*, © The Delegates of the Oxford University Press 1961 and 1970, and are used by permission.

Scripture quotations designated JB are from *The Jerusalem Bible*, copyright © 1966 by Darton, Longman & Todd, Ltd. and Doubleday & Company, Inc. Used by per-mission of the publishers.

Scripture quotations designated AP are the author's paraphrase.

Scripture quotations designated PA are from *Psalms Anew* by Nancy Schreck and Maureen Leach, published by Saint Mary's Press, copyright 1986 by Saint Mary's Press, and are used by permission.

Excerpt from *Mister God, This Is Anna* by Fynn, copyright © Fynn 1974, published by William Collins Sons & Co., is used by permission.

Excerpt from A RAISIN IN THE SUN by Lorraine Hansberry. Copyright © 1958 by Robert Nemiroff as an unpublished work. Copyright © 1959, 1966, 1984 by Robert Nemiroff. Reprinted by permission of Random House, Inc.

Lines reprinted with permission of Macmillan Publishing Company and of Macmillan, London, and Basingstoke from FIREFLIES by Rathindranath Tagore. Copyright 1928 by Macmillan Publishing Company, renewed 1955 Rathindranath Tagore.

Excerpt from *Meditations of the Heart* by Howard Thurman. Published by Friends United Press, © 1976. Used by permission.

Excerpt reprinted by permission from ACTION INFORMATION published by The Alban Institute, Inc., 4125 Nebraska Avenue, NW, Washington, DC 20016. Copy-right 1980. All rights reserved.

Cover Design: Karen Horner/Jackson Design
First Printing: April 1988 (10)
Second Printing: November 1989 (7)
Third Printing: July 1991 (3)
Fourth Printing: March 1992 (5)
Library of Congress Catalog Card Number: 87-051425
ISBN: 0-8358-0582-4

Printed in the United States of America

For Larry
steadfast and supportive as we share the spirit journey

CONTENTS

JOURNALING

A Spirit Journey

An Introduction to Journaling

The indomitable Grandma Bagley, in a story called "Maggie's Journal," gives a journal to a young girl who faces a summer in bed with a broken leg. Grandma tells her:

It's a journal, Maggie, a special place for you to put down all the special things you think or see or dream, anytime you want. When you are in a rotten mood and your brain is full of cobwebs, or when life is so marvelous you feel like you're soaring in a balloon, you can put it all down in your journal. You can go through your own looking-glass, Maggie, and find your wonderland. . . .

All kinds of things happen during the day, but sometimes you don't notice them because you aren't paying attention. Writing in your journal helps you see things you never thought about before. You notice the way honeysuckle smells after the rain and the lacy pattern the moonlight makes on your ceiling when you lie in bed at night. Soon, each day seems full of small marvels you must write down.

For this young girl, the journal became a forum for "feelings of sadness and fear and joy and wonder in the

11

small world of her room" that would "remind her always of the summer in which some things were lost but many more were discovered."[1]

Journaling is about discovering. Throughout the ages, men and women have kept a record of their lives. Toward the beginning of time, drawings scratched into the side of caves left a record of that early life. Records were also kept orally through stories repeated from generation to generation. As civilization progressed, people began writing down their thoughts and experiences, their personal and corporate history. For centuries, people have discovered new things about themselves and their world through journaling.

These records or journals were kept for various reasons. Some individuals saw themselves as historians, chronicling life at their point in history. Others kept a journal for their personal use. Perhaps their writing (and the rereading of those words) helped them chart progress or reach life-goals. Whatever the reason for keeping a journal or diary, many have found it to be a rewarding discipline.

WHY JOURNAL?

There is a difference between a diary and a journal. A diary is a record of daily events in one's own life. The journal may take as its starting point the same events as a diary, but in journaling, one looks inward to see how one is affected by the events.

In a diary one might record, "I went to see *The Color Purple*." A journal would go deeper into feelings and reflections on the person's experience. "I went to see *The Color Purple*. I became really involved in the movie and identified with Celie. As she began to like and see herself in a new way, I, too, felt empowered. How have I been oppressed? How am I becoming my true self?"

Each of us carries on inner conversations as we sort through our feelings about daily living, our relationships, world events. Journaling is the process of writing down those "talks with ourselves" so that what our mind is thinking and our heart is feeling becomes tangible: ink on paper.

Putting one's life down on paper is often helpful as a clarifying process: Who am I? What am I doing and why? How do I feel about my life, my world? In what ways am I growing or changing?

One journaler says, "There's something about actually putting words on paper that clears my mind. As I think through what I want to say, I realize what I'm feeling. And somehow I feel better. I hear what I'm saying just as if I were talking to a friend."

JOURNALING AS SPIRITUAL DISCIPLINE

Journaling can be more than simply a means to "think things through"; it can be a spiritual discipline. One person may journal in response to Bible study. Another may take a meditational walk or have a time of silence and then record the thoughts and prayers that occurred during that time. Someone else may record daily events and then see the hand of God in that dailiness. Journaling can be a freeing spiritual discipline because there is no set "right" method for spiritual growth, but a variety of approaches that have in common pen, paper, and the desire to come closer to God in the writing.

God is active in the world and in our lives in many ways. We may feel the mystery of God as we view storm clouds brewing over a blue ocean. We may experience the love of God when we are comforted by a friend. We may be filled with the compassion of God as we attend a conference on the plight of the homeless. We may be blessed by the peace of God during prayer or troubled by the challenges of God as we study the Bible. God comes to us in both our conscious and our unconscious experiences, for God is in all of life.

There are times when God's activity seems clear: in a

specifically answered prayer, the saving of a seemingly unredeemable situation, strength that is wondrously given at just the right moment. At other times we recognize God's interaction with us only in hindsight—when we take time to reflect on our lives.

Journaling provides us with a means of reflection. We are gifted with a space and time to open ourselves to the Lover of the World. Journaling is a private discipline in which we can reveal ourselves totally. There is no need to carefully consider words or wonder what other people might think of our thoughts. Journal-writing is a sharing between our true selves and the God of Truth. In journaling, we come to know ourselves as we really are and feel the acceptance of the One who loves us no matter what.

Journaling becomes spiritual discipline when we use pen and paper to strengthen our faith in God. We can use journaling as a companion to prayer, Bible study, fasting, or any other spiritual discipline that is already part of our life in God. Journaling can be a significant tool in deepening our spiritual lives because by its nature it leads us to further revelation of who we are and who God is in our lives.

Journaling: A Spirit Journey will present a sampler of journaling methods for spiritual growth. Six possible approaches to spiritual journaling will be outlined within a structure that helps the journaler try out each method for one week. *Journaling: A Spirit Journey* can be used by individuals or groups as a mini-course in spiritual journaling. At the end of six weeks, the journaler will know which methods are most helpful in his or her personal journey of faith. An epilogue will give ideas for further growth and journaling.

Here is an overview of the six methods:

1. God most often meets us in the mundane details of our daily lives. Do we recognize the Risen Christ in our dishwashing, bill paying, or tucking the kids in at night? Do we feel God's presence as we write to our legislators or

march for peace? Journaling the events of our lives can help us see God in all of life.

2. The Bible is our base, the touchstone of our faith. Journaling in response to scripture helps us be formed by God's word as well as informed in our study. Rather than being spectators watching the biblical story unfold, we are active participants in that story.

3. Guided meditations take us on a journey deep into our psyche where imagination plays with reality. On this journey, we often come in touch with the God who lives at all levels of our consciousness. Such meditations are specifically designed to bring us closer to God in new understanding.

4. Dreams are a special gift of our sleeping hours. Through these subconscious experiences we can sometimes find needed meaning in our waking. God the Dreamer may also speak to us in our daydreams, guiding us to vision, then to live out our lives in the world as they are meant to be.

5. Our daily times of reading (newspapers, magazines, books) can be the basis for dialogue with ourselves and God. Do certain passages jump out at us? Such passages are a fertile ground for discovering the God within us as we interact with them.

6. Most people engage in dozens of conversations each day. Whether we are talking with family, friends, business acquaintances, or strangers, God may speak to us through these seemingly ordinary conversations.

These six methods are only a beginning, options among many possibilities for journaling. It is not necessary to follow the suggested order; each chapter, with its particular method of journaling, stands alone. So if you are most interested in journaling with scripture, go straight to chapter 2. If you feel drawn to explore your dreams through journaling, let chapter 4 be your starting point. You may want to explore all six methods. You may quickly find the method that best suits your needs and temperament; or you may discover your own style of journaling, using bits and pieces of other methods. Feel free to use this book in whatever way will be of most help to you in your own spirit journey.

Each chapter contains blank pages for your own personal journaling. You might find it helpful to date each entry; there may be times later when you will return to read of this time in your life. The pages are blank so you can custom-fit your own writing size and style to the beckoning whiteness. Do not feel limited to one page per day. Undoubtedly, there will be days when you have greater need to write.

In this high-tech age, it may seem most practical to use a tape recorder rather than actually writing in a journal. Can the same thing not be accomplished by speaking into a tape recorder while driving to work? Certainly, commuting time can be put to good spiritual-growth use. However, there are definite advantages to putting pen to paper to record your growth in Christ. First, a journal is more accessible. If you want to reread an entry from a certain point in your life, it will be easier to look through the pages of a journal than to listen to hours of a cassette tape. Tape-recorded messages, unless transcribed to written form, are limiting.

Second, there is something in the physical act of writing that releases creativity and self-understanding. Spiritual growth is not just a verbal matter. In journaling, your hands can lead you to new insights because they can write, doodle, draw—can give a variety of expressions to what you are thinking and feeling. Journaling allows you to use both right-brain and left-brain skills.

Focusing on one thing (writing in your journal) rather than making journaling a time-efficient activity allows you to concentrate on God's presence single-mindedly.

GETTING STARTED

"I began these pages for myself, in order to think out my own particular pattern of living, my own individual balance of life, work, and human relationships. And since I think best with a pencil in my hand, I started naturally to write."[2] So Anne Morrow Lindbergh began her famous *Gift from the Sea*. She knew that the writing itself would help her put her life in perspective. You who are about to begin journaling as a discipline of the Christian faith know that taking pen to paper may lead to a clearer understanding of who you are in relation to the One whose death on the cross puts all things in perspective.

Most people do not consider themselves writers. "Writing" conjures up images of high-school term papers, famous novelists, or the amusing newspaper columnist you read in the daily newspaper. Yet whatever your image of "writing," feel assured that in your private journal, your own style is the best possible. You need to know how to write words on paper, but it does not matter if the writing is legible (other than to you) or if the spelling and punctuation are perfect. All that matters is that you seek a closer relationship to the God of Life and that you are ready to try journaling as a spiritual discipline.

As a child of God, you have infinite worth. Your words, even your descriptions of what may seem to be very ordinary things to you, are unique and important. The more you journal, the more comfortable you will be with the process of putting words on paper. You may be surprised at your growing creativity: journaling unlocks the imagination.

To start, you need to choose a journal. Some people prefer a simple spiral notebook with lined pages. Others enjoy a blank-paged book with a cover and style all their own. Size, weight, and price are practical considerations. It is important, however, to have a separate journal that can be a permanent record of your spiritual growth. This journal will become a friend, one of the first possessions to be saved in case of fire, for this friend will know more of your inner life than most people will.

Try to find a pen or pencil that has a feel and look you like. On different days, you may feel like writing in bold black or fine-lined blue or faint pencil; it is up to you. Any notebook and writing implement will do; when you feel good about your particular journal and pen or pencil, the process of journaling will seem more beckoning.

For most people, a specific time to journal helps this action become a discipline. Perhaps you will want to get up and journal in the quiet of early morning. Or you may find that journaling just before bedtime helps you "take your rest in God." If you wake in the night and find it hard to go back to sleep, journaling might be most fruitful then. Maybe there is a lull or quiet time in the middle of your day (or maybe you can make that needed space) that will be best for journaling. The time is not important; *regularity* of journaling is.

Some places make it easier to focus on the journaling process. Do you have a favorite chair in the living room? At home or at work, is there a room where you can find privacy? Do you best focus on God in the beauty of your backyard? Experiment until you find the place that best lends itself to the discipline of journaling.

Even when you have settled on a journal, writing tool, time, and place, there will be those other moments when you are unexpectedly gifted with the time or need to write. If you do not have your journal with you, find any sort of paper and pen or pencil. Give thanks for the time and then write; you can transfer your thoughts to your regular journal later. You may find God in a new way while sitting in the doctor's office or waiting for a bus. If your life has many such moments, you might want to consider buying an especially portable journal and making it a point to take it with you wherever you go.

So now you have your journal and pen, have chosen a time and place, and are ready to sit down to write. Take a few moments to relax and prepare yourself for God's spirit to work within you in this time of journaling. Breathe deeply. Pray that the time may be fruitful and that you may know God more fully in your writing. You will find your own ways of clearing your mind of other things so that you are ready to give full attention to God, who can speak to you through your journaling.

If distractions come—and at first they may fly at you fast and furious—keep a piece of scratch paper nearby so that you can jot down a word that will remind you enough of them that you can deal with them later. Items for the grocery list, necessary phone calls, projects due can then be put aside during your journaling time.

Having prepared yourself for journaling, commit yourself to the six-week process of trying out this book's sampler of journaling methods. Each week's method will have its own feel and style. Some will feel immediately comfortable; others may take longer to find your rhythm. If a given method feels uncomfortable, try it out for a week before you disregard it completely. The advantage of trying out all six methods is that you will see the great varieties of approaches to journaling and then discover which methods are most helpful to you in your personal spiritual journey.

The epilogue will help you evaluate your six-week growth in journaling and look to the future for further implementation of the journaling discipline.

Those of you who will experience the format of *Journaling: A Spirit Journey* as a group will need to discuss meeting place and time. Your group might choose one leader per week to begin the sharing time: How have I grown closer to God this week through this journaling method? What have I learned of myself? of God? At what point did I find difficulty? In which parts of the journaling has there been a sense of fulfillment? It is important to foster an atmosphere of trust in which group members feel comfortable sharing and also feel accepted if they choose not to share.

Whether you undertake your journaling discipline alone or in a group, you are placing yourself in the presence of the Living God who is interested in all aspects of our lives. Howard Thurman reminds us that God is ever ready to meet us even as we venture forth to establish a closer tie with the Almighty.

Again and again I am conscious that I am seeking God. There is ever present in me a searching, longing for some ultimate resting place for my spirit—some final haven of refuge from storms and upheavals of life. I seek ever the kind of peace that can pervade my total life, ... covering me completely with a vast tranquility. This I seek not because I am a coward, not because I am afraid of life or of living, but because the urge seems to steady me to the very core.

With sustained excitement, I recall what, in my own urgency, I had forgotten: God is seeking me. Blessed remembrance! God is seeking me. Wonderful assurance; God is seeking me. This is the meaning of my longing, this is the warp of my desiring, this is my point. The searching that keeps the sand hot under my feet is but my response to His seeking. Therefore, this moment, I will be still, I will quiet my reaching out, I will abide; for to know really that God is seeking me; to be aware of the NOW is to be found of Him. Then, as if by a miracle, He becomes the answer to my need. It sufficeth now and forever that *I am* found of Him.

God is seeking me this moment.[3]

NOTES

1. Ethel Marbach, "Maggie's Journal," *Pockets*, July 1985, pp. 13-14.

2. Anne Morrow·Lindbergh, *Gift From the Sea* (New York: Random House, 1978), p. 9.

3. Howard Thurman, *Meditations of the Heart* (New York: Harper & Brothers, 1953), pp. 175-176.

One

Journaling from the Events of Daily Life

When I was eight I was given my first diary. I faithfully entered a few lines most days, carefully locking the special book and hiding it when I had completed my entry. My diary writing reflected who I was at that point in my life; entries were simple and concerned my friends, pets, church, school.

I continued the practice of keeping a diary through junior and senior high school. As I reread these diary entries, it is easy to see what was most important: my blossoming interest in boys. Only to the secret diary friend could I divulge who I liked, how I felt when a particular boy talked to me, whose hand I held in the closing church youth group circle. Little by little, I wrote more of my inner life, again sharing details I would never have spoken out loud to friends or family.

In college I began the transition to journal-writing. My entries no longer simply listed the events of my life. I began to look deep within myself to see how I was being affected by my life. My experience as "assistant to the pastors" at my local church led me to use the pages of my journal to think through my call to ministry. In response to my philosophy course, I wrote long sections on being a philosophical "rationalist." My relationships with various young men caused me to write down how I perceived myself; I evaluated my behavior, searched for role possibilities as a woman, began to learn who I was within and outside of such relationships.

More and more I used the journal as a place to discover and rediscover who I was: woman, scholar, Christian, friend. By the time I began a journal specifically titled "Pondering Motherhood," I saw my journaling as a way to think through life decisions. Not only did I include ideas and quotes from readings or conversations, but I carried on a dialogue—with myself, with God—stimulated by the actions and events of my life.

At this point in my life, my journal expands those inner dialogues to prayerful contemplation not just on my own life but on the world around me. How is God speaking to me through the newspaper photo of a disaster victim, the arms limitation talks, my daughter's questions, the disturbing telephone call from a parishioner? What am I to do with those recurring thoughts that seem to be God's gentle but persistent nudgings? How, in all the myriad of daily activities, do I keep track of Whose I am?

Journaling from the events of daily life does not mean simply keeping a log or diary of who we saw and what we did each day. It means, rather, writing down the experiences that have affected our soul in a particular way. We may experience a hectic and strained day at work and, in journaling, consider if what we are doing has any meaning. We may see our grandmother in a nursing home and begin thinking not only of what our own life will be like when she dies but also of our own mortality, our belief in eternal life, the questions we would like to ask God.

Unlike keeping a diary, journaling does not cause us to focus simply on what is at hand; rather, it frees us to explore the rooms hidden in our hearts, making meaning of our lives. We do not just chronicle how we have acted; we open up and explore our reactions to our world and how God is at work in all the aspects of our lives.

In journaling we can clarify why we do what we do, in what ways we live out our faith. God most often meets us in the ordinary details of our lives. Do we recognize the Risen Christ there? How does our faith affect decisions made at work or how we relate to our family? Journaling the events of our lives can help us see God in all of life.

In *Journal of a Solitude*, May Sarton writes:

> We have to make myths of our own lives, the point being that if we do, then every grief or inexplicable seizure by weather, woe, or work can—if we discipline ourselves and think hard enough—be turned to account, be made to yield further insight into what it is to be alive, to be a human being, what the hazards are of a fairly usual, everyday kind. We go up to Heaven and down to Hell a dozen times a day—at least, I do. And the discipline of work provides an exercise bar, so that the wild, irrational motions of the soul become formal and creative.[1]

Sarton reminds us that regularly looking into our "usual, everyday lives" can guide us into growth of the soul as we take stock of who we are. Where do I put most of my energy? How would I chart my emotions for a particular day or week? Are there patterns to my behavior? Where does my faith in God enter into all the intricate aspects of my life? In what concrete ways have I felt touched by the presence of God? How am I affected by a seeming absence of my Creator?

We should use our own day-to-day experience as one guideline in decision-making. John Wesley's "quadralateral" links scripture, tradition, reason, and experience as a four-fold lens on life. Doug Wingeier, in his *Working Out Your Own Beliefs* writes: "Any experience can be a religious experience. All that prevents it from being so is our blindness to the presence of God in it. The regular practice of making theological meaning out of our experience will help us transform ordinary events into meetings with God. Like Moses, we will be able to hear God speaking to us from a plain, ordinary bush and be led to take off our shoes, 'for the place on which you are standing is holy ground' (Exodus 3:5."[2]

A DAILY ROUTINE FOR JOURNALING
FROM THE EVENTS OF DAILY LIFE

This week we will journal in response to our own life experience. Each day, after you have chosen your place and time to journal, take a few minutes to center yourself by sitting quietly, breathing deeply, saying a breath prayer. Then gently think over your day—its events, people, places. (If you have chosen an early morning journaling time, consider the events of the previous day.) Remember that this day's activities are the starting point for reflection; you may want to write some details of a particular incident as it affected you, but you probably will not list the chronology of your day.

After you have thought through the day's events, ask yourself the following questions to start the day's journaling, using the blank pages provided at the end of this chapter:
• How am I feeling about myself? my world?
• Where today did I specifically see or feel the presence of God working in my life and in the world?
• Was I aware of God at the time? If not, what attitudes or actions were blocking my receptiveness to the Divine?
• In what ways was I able to bring the spirit of Christ to the various parts of my life? How did I fail to show his loving spirit and compassion?
• Were there specific events this day that helped me understand who I am as a follower of Christ?

OTHER WAYS TO GET STARTED

If none of these questions sparks ideas, consider the following:

• Is there a conversation or event that you feel the need to look at more carefully? Do you have unresolved feelings about what someone said or did? Have you been continuing a conversation with someone in your mind, thinking of words you wish you had said or an action you wish you had taken? What might God be asking you to consider through this conversation or event?

• Was there a time when you felt a strong emotion (joy, anger, hurt, concern, disappointment, pride)? Why might this emotion have surfaced? How do you picture the Giver of All Feelings responding to you as you experience this emotion?

• Are there things you would like to say to God in response to this day? Questions or thank-yous or explanations may feel appropriate as you seek to come closer to the God of All Days.

If your particular day's experiences do not seem to fit into any of these categories, you might want to start by completing any of the following thoughts in a free-flowing (stream-of-consciousness) style.

My life is...

I am...

To me, God is...

My need for God shows when...

I feel God may be calling me to...

Just listing responses to these kinds of questions may help you flow into a routine of using your daily experience as impetus for journaling.

Another way to get started in daily-experience journaling is to use your journal pages to write down a letter from God. Considering what is going on in your life at this point, what might God say to you? Do you need to hear a message of forgiveness or hope? Might God call you to repentance and accountability?

As you try out different approaches to this daily-life journaling, you will become more comfortable with simply sitting down and reflecting on the day's events, using your journal pages to see how your life reflects the power of God. Your life is a gift of God; journaling about your specific life-experience can be a channel to understanding more clearly how God is working in the details that make up your day.

RESOURCES FOR FURTHER JOURNALING IN RESPONSE TO DAILY LIFE

There are many fine examples of personal journals—books that show the writer's developing inner life as he or she responds to the world. Here is a sampling of such journals, each of which could provide impetus for your own daily-life journaling.

The Measure of My Days by Florida Scott-Maxwell (Alfred A. Knopf, 1968) was written by an eighty-two-year-old woman surveying her own life and the journey of humanity in the twentieth century.

Bring Me a Unicorn (Harcourt Brace Jovanovich, 1972), *War Within and Without* (Harcourt Brace Jovanovich, 1980), *Hour of Gold, Hour of Lead* (Harcourt Brace Jovanovich, 1973) and other journal books by Anne Morrow Lindbergh. Balancing her very public life as Charles Lindbergh's wife, Anne used her journal as a way to work through her roles of mother, wife, writer.

Journal of a Solitude (W. W. Norton, 1973) by May Sarton. Novelist and poet May Sarton writes of her daily life in New Hampshire: the garden, changing seasons, friends, spiritual journey.

The Province Beyond the River: The Diary of a Protestant at a Trappist Monastery (The Upper Room, 1986) by W. Paul Jones. This book journals the months spent by the author at a remote monastery where he discovered God and himself in a new way.

The Color Purple (Washington Square Books, 1982) by Alice Walker. In this fictional work, Celie writes a series of letters that function much as a journal in recording the events of this main character's life—letters that help her make sense of what is happening to her.

Quaker Journals: Varieties of Religious Experience among Friends (Pendle Hill Publications, 1983) is edited by Howard Brinton. The "varieties of religious experience among Friends" is explored through selections from early Quaker journals.

The Hermitage Journals (Doubleday, 1983) by John Howard Griffin is the diary he kept while working on the biography of Trappist monk Thomas Merton.

An Interrupted Life: The Diaries of Etty Hillesum (Pantheon Books, 1984). Living in Amsterdam during the Nazi occupation, this young Jewish woman wrote of her love, friends, fears, hopes before she was taken to Auschwitz.

Genesee Diary (Doubleday, 1976) by Henri Nouwen. A seven-month stay at a Trappist monastery is chronicled in terms of the author's spiritual growth. His *¡Gracias! A Latin American Journal* (Harper and Row, 1983) records his six-month stay in Bolivia and Peru.

The Crosswicks Journal Trilogy (Seabury Press, 1972) (*A Circle of Quiet, The Summer of the Great-Grandmother, The Irrational Season*) by Madeleine L'Engle are composed from her daily journaling, though they are not in journal form.

NOTES

1. May Sarton, *Journal of a Solitude* (New York: W. W. Norton, 1973), pp. 108-109.

2. Doug Wingeier, *Working Out Your Own Beliefs* (Nashville: Abingdon, 1980), p. 40.

JOURNALING FROM THE EVENTS OF DAILY LIFE

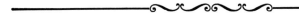

Two

Journaling in Response to Scripture

Harriett's family did not go to church. Once when she was ten years old she went to the Baptist Sunday school with a friend. She still clearly remembers the scripture lesson. To illustrate the story of Moses in the bulrushes, the teacher used a sandbox table to create an actual river complete with tiny reeds and rushes that the children helped position in the scene. There were small cardboard figures dressed appropriately and, of course, a tiny baby Moses housed safely in his basket.

Fifty years later, Harriett is an active laywoman. The Bible is an important part of her life. And the story of Moses, so vividly portrayed for seven Iowa children in a Baptist Sunday school class, remains real and important to her. She feels the power of the Bible as it touches her life and can affirm, with John Wesley, "O give me that book! At any price, give me the book of God!...Here is knowledge enough for me."[1]

The stories of the Bible mean the most to us when they are truly a part of us. We understand ourselves and our world better when we feel touched by the loving God who has sought and continues to seek humanity throughout history. When we are able to enter fully into a passage of scripture, we deeply comprehend the love and understanding of our Creator.

As we begin to comprehend God's love, we cannot help but be changed. That we could be loved so much! That God's love can flow through us to others! Walter Wink writes that the goal of Bible study is "the transformation of persons toward the divine possibilities inherent in them." Wink details this transformation that can happen when we give ourselves to the power of the Bible:

> Transformation involves the movement from egocentric control of one's life toward a life centered on commitment to the will of God, whatever that might entail and however costly it might turn out to be. It is exploring all the sealed and stale rooms of this God's house we call our selves, and offering all we find to the real owner for forgiveness, acceptance, and healing. It is unmasking our complicity in systems and structures of society which violate people's lives, and becoming ready agents of justice. It is discovering the unjust and violated parts of ourselves as well. It is a process, not an arriving: we are "transforming," not transformed. But all along the way there are flashes of insight, moments of exquisite beauty, experiences of forgiveness and of being healed, reconciliations and revelations that confirm the rightness of our quest and whet our appetites for more.[2]

The quest is for closeness to God. The Bible, in its rich variety, tells of other persons in other times who were transformed by God's power working in their lives. How can we learn from their experience? How do we come closer to the God of past, present, and future through the lives of Noah or Deborah, Jeremiah or Elizabeth? In what ways can the Bible come alive for us so that we feel the presence of the Living God?

One of the classic ways of reading the Bible comes to us from the monastic tradition. Throughout the centuries, the monastic community has followed the rhythm of prayer, work, and study (*ora, labora, lectio divina*). The monks studied the Bible using *lectio divina*—"divine reading."

> The vital feature of this discipline is not what one studies but how one studies it. The approach is a slow, thoughtful, prayerful dialogue with the material, grounded in the faith that behind the words we read there is always a Word to encounter.
>
> We have been schooled to study for information; in *lectio* we study for insight. We have learned how to study to "master" a field; in *lectio* we study so the truth might master us. In the academy we study with our minds, always analyzing and dissecting; in *lectio* we do not abandon the mind but let it descend into the heart, where the "hidden wholeness" of things may be discovered again. Normally, we read and question the text; in *lectio* we allow that text to read and question us.[3]

Lectio divina is a contemplative study of the Bible, a way to intimately interact with the word of God. M. Robert Mulholland calls this "formational reading" of the Bible that allows the reader to interact with scripture. As Mulholland writes:

> Formational reading is in depth. You are seeking to allow the passage to open out to you its deeper dynamics, its multiple layers of meaning. Instead of rushing on to the next sentence, paragraph, or chapter, you seek to move deeper and deeper and deeper into the text. In reading the Bible, for example, you seek to allow the text to begin to become that intrusion of the Word of God into your life, to address you, to encounter you. If you don't take time with a text, the Word cannot encounter you in it; the Word of God cannot speak to you through it.[4]

One way to deeply interact with the word of God in a formational way is to read a scripture passage and then journal in response to the word. The act of journaling brings about an intimate relationship between the reader-journaler and the biblical story. The reader is pulled from informational "head-reading" to formational interaction: What is the word of God specifically saying to me?

The Bible has been guiding God-seeking people throughout the centuries. Individuals have found different verses or stories to be helpful to them in their spiritual pilgrimages. The Bible can be most formational when viewed as a continuing story. Old Testament books narrate the story of the people of Israel and their relationship to God. The New Testament tells of the life of Jesus and how his resurrection affected the early church. And the love story of God and humanity does not end with the last page of the Bible. God is ever-creating, ever-interacting in today's world as well—the story continues.

One of the characters in *The Winter of Our Discontent* by john Steinbeck knew the power of the continuing God-story in her life. Aunt Deborah "read the Scripture to me like a daily newspaper and I suppose that's the way she thought of it, as something going on happening eternally but always exciting and new. Every Easter, Jesus really rose from the dead, an explosion, expected but nonetheless new. It wasn't two thousand years ago to her; it was now."[5]

How is Jesus' resurrection affecting your present life? How does the biblical story interact with your own story (past, present, and future)? In what ways is God speaking to you today? Journaling can help you focus on questions such as these that apply to you even as they applied to Abraham, Esther, Mary Magdalene, Paul, and Christians throughout the centuries.

This week you will have the opportunity to try journaling in response to scripture. For each day of the week, there will be a scripture passage to experience, then some questions to begin the journaling process. As you read, remember that the goal is not to read a certain amount of words from the Bible or to analyze all the meanings of the text. The goal of journaling with scripture is to understand the word of God as it intimately relates to you. If twenty verses are suggested and if you are particularly struck by what the third verse says, take time to let God speak to you through that verse. It might be a window to your relationship with the Divine Mystery, bringing you closer to God this day.

Use whatever translation is most helpful to you. Looking at two or more translations of a particular passage gives the chance to perceive its subtle nuances. You might want to read from *Today's English Version*, the Revised Standard Version, and *The Jerusalem Bible*, for instance. If you enjoy the easy reading of *The Living Bible* (a paraphrase, not a translation), always use a translation in conjunction with it so you can have a true rendering of the original Hebrew, Aramaic, or Greek as well as simple language.

The following suggestions may be useful as you prepare to journal in response to scripture:

1. Take a few moments to relax and clear your mind of any distractions. Breathe deeply. Pray that this time might be an opening to God's spirit. Sense the possibilities of your time of journaling.

2. Find the day's selected scripture passage. Read any instructions.

3. Read the selected passage of scripture slowly. Try to visualize its images.

4. Read the passage again. You might want to jot down any ideas, questions, key phrases that come to you as you read.

5. Open your journal and begin writing on the blank pages, using the printed questions as a starting point. Let your writing flow naturally. Spelling and grammar are not important. Writing your deepest responses to God's word is what counts.

6. Consider: What might God be saying specifically to me in this passage?

7. When you feel a sense of closure to your writing (or have finished your allotted time), take time to thank God

for these words of scripture and what you can learn of the continuing God-story through the Bible.

The week's scripture verses focus on God and God's action in our lives. An overview of the daily themes reminds us of the Creator's incredible love and power:

Day One: God Is Our Shelter and Strength
Day Two: God Is Love
Day Three: God's Love Is Forever
Day Four: God Makes All Things New
Day Five: God Transforms Our Weakness
Day Six: God Provides for All Our Needs
Day Seven: God Answers Prayer

Each day's interaction with scripture will be different. There will be suggestions of various techniques to try as you read God's word. Open yourself to God's leading. Let God's spirit be your guide. May this week of journaling bring you closer to the God who is everything to us.

Day One: God Is Our Shelter and Strength (Psalm 46)

> God is our refuge and our strength,
> our ever-present help in distress.
> —Psalm 46:1, PA

Read Psalm 46, using more than one translation if possible. How would you put the theme of this psalm into one sentence? Or could you write a paraphrase of the psalm that would personalize it for you?

This psalm affirms God's power: we can count on our Maker to care for us even through earthquakes and floods (vv. 3, 4) or wars and conflicts (v. 6). The repeated chorus (vv. 7, 11) proclaims, "The Lord of hosts is with us; the God of Jacob is our refuge." Each verse gives further evidence of God's steadfastness. Our God stands firm in the midst of the holy river, does marvelous things on earth, is exalted. Most importantly, the Most High is with us.

Take time to write down some of the fears you may have.

Do you fear tornadoes? nuclear holocaust? harm to your children? approaching old age? Write your own affirmation of God's power, such as "Even in the midst of tornadoes and storms, God is with me" or "Though I may fear the possibility of nuclear devastation, I trust in God to care for me."

This is a passage full of strong visual images. You might want to try drawing some of the verses in your journal— just simple line drawings, particularly verses 2, 3, 4, 5, 6, and 9. As you illustrate the biblical passage, the words may come alive for you in a new way.

Day Two: God Is Love (1 John 4:7-21)

> Dear friends, if this is how God loved us,
> then we should love one another.
> —1 John 4:11, TEV

Before you read the scripture passage, put the word *love* in your journal. Underneath, write words or phrases that come into your mind associated with love. If a visual image comes to mind, draw that picture or use words to describe it. Feel free to fill up a page or more, if needed, to make a word and picture collage on love.

Next, read through 1 John 4:7-21. This passage focuses on love—in these few verses, *Today's English Version* lists love in varied forms twenty-seven times. In your journal, add to your love collage any new understandings or images of love that come to you from this passage.

Reread verses 7-10. Put these verses into your own words on the journal page. How did and does God show love? How do we fit into God's plan of love?

Read verses 11-16 again. "If this is how God loved us, then we should love one another." In your own life, what are some concrete ways in which you can and do show love? Do you feel yourself a channel of the divine love? In your own spirit journey, how do you know and believe the love which God has for us?

Look again at verses 19-21. Think a minute about the logic of "someone cannot love God, who hasn't been seen, if that person doesn't love a neighbor, who has been seen" (ap). Are there individuals you have difficulty in loving? Write their names in the journal. Let your words flow onto the page in prayer. Ask for whatever you need from God to receive God's gift of the love that can overcome all personality conflicts, misunderstandings, barriers, and walls. As you write, feel the incredible love described in 1 John 4, and know that such a love is available to you.

Day Three: God's Love Is Forever (Romans 8:31-39)

> Who shall separate us from the love of Christ?
> —Romans 8:35

Read the suggested verses, then answer the following questions in your journal:
• Have there been times when you have felt separated from God? Have you experienced trouble, hardship, persecution, hunger, poverty, danger, or death? Were you able to feel God's presence during these times?
• Read verse 38 several times. Say these words as an affirmation of faith. How do you feel when you know that nothing "will be able to separate us from the love of God in Christ Jesus our Lord"? What does it mean to you that God was made visible in Jesus?

Day Four: God Makes All Things New (Isaiah 43:16-21)

> Behold, I am doing a new thing.
> —Isaiah 43:19

Read this passage, then reread it, focusing on the verses by pairs.
1. Verses 16-17 recall Israel's deliverance from oppression in Egypt. This was a key event in the history of Israel;

God's power was visibly manifest at a crucial point in the Hebrews' escape from the pursuing Egyptian army.
• When has God's power been made manifest to you in a dramatic way? How did you feel? How does the memory of this time strengthen you now?

2. In *The Jerusalem Bible*, verse 18 is translated as "No need to recall the past, no need to think about what was done before."
• What events in your live are still influencing how you relate to the present? Can you let go of any of the past's hurts? How do God's forgiveness and acceptance free you to live out today with a clean slate?

"Behold, I am doing a new thing; . . . do you not perceive it?"
• What new thing is God doing in your life? How can you be most open to God's positive action in you?

3. The animals join humanity in singing praises for the gift of water in the wilderness (verses 20-21).
• How do you experience the rivers of life? In what ways do you give praise?

Day Five: God Transforms Our Weakness (Luke 13:10-17)

> Immediately she was made straight, and she praised God.
> —Luke 13:13

Before reading the scripture passage, spend three minutes walking around bent over in half. Imagine yourself talking to people you meet on the street. How does it feel to relate to others from this stance? Can you imagine always looking down instead of up?

When the three minutes are up, do some stretches to relax your back. Stand straight and stretch to the sky. Then bend forward until your head is hanging relaxed to the floor. Feel the strength of a healthy back before relaxing into your time of journaling.

If physical restrictions make it impossible for you to take

the three minutes of bent-over time, close your eyes and visualize yourself in that position. Perhaps your own restrictions will be a gift to you in understanding this passage.

After reading the verses of scripture, consider these questions:

1. Think of the woman who spent eighteen years bent over in a spirit of infirmity. How was her vision narrowed? What possibilities would have been closed to her?

2. When Jesus responds to the remarks of the ruler of the synagogue (v. 16), what is he saying about the worth of this woman?

3. Many things can bend one's back: loneliness, injustice, hopelessness, resentment, oppression, despair. In your own life, what is it that causes your back to bend? How would you identify the bent-over part of yourself? What might be your spirit of infirmity?

4. In your journal, write a prayer to Jesus, detailing your own infirmity (weakness, failing). Share your feelings honestly, knowing that you will be heard. Take a few moments of silence. Then write what Jesus might say to you, as he said to the woman bent over for eighteen years: "Woman, you are freed from your frailty."

Day Six: God Provides for All Our Needs (Luke 12:22-31)

Therefore, I tell you, do not be anxious about your life.
—Luke 12:22

Before you read today's scripture verses, make a list in your journal of what things you really need in order to exist. Some might be tangibles such as food and shelter; others might be the need of love or of being appreciated. Try to separate those things you might want (financial security, a bigger house) from what you actually need.

Then read today's scripture passage as if Jesus were speaking directly to you. Let yourself see and experience the wonderful visual images he presents of birds, flowers,

and grass. Then use some of the following questions as food for thought in journaling:
• What is the central message in what Jesus is saying?
• How is he encouraging his listeners to have faith in God?
• When he says, "Instead, be concerned with God's reign, and God will give you everything you need" (v. 31, AP) what does he mean?
• In your own life, are there things about which you feel anxious? Write down any worries that are presently bothering you. Be honest; lift up these worries to the One who understands your every preoccupation even as God also meets your every need. Let your words be a prayer that you might trust God more and rely on yourself less, appreciating the many gifts you already have.

If it feels hard to "let go and let God," you might list those gifts already present in your life. Give thanks for your family and friends, food and shelter, material possessions and moments of peace of mind—whatever God has already gifted you with.

Day Seven: God Answers Prayer (Mark 10:46-52)

> Master, let me receive my sight.
> —Mark 10:51

Read the passage twice, visualizing the scene as it unfolds. Then close your Bible and tell the story out loud as you remember it. Open your Bible to see if you forgot any important details. Now tell the story again, this time from the perspective of Bartimaeus. Use the first person ("I") as you recount his healing. Imagine your emotions as you sit by the roadside, hear Jesus coming, shout for attention. Hear the crowd scolding you for shouting. Jump up to meet Jesus. Feel the power of his asking, "What do you want me to do for you?" Be blind Bartimaeus asserting your desire. Receive your sight. Picture your life changing after this miracle. What will it mean to no longer be a beggar? How will you "follow him on the way"?

In your journal, write how it felt to become Bartimaeus. How are you like him? How do you feel the power of Christ?

Answer Jesus' question, "What do you want me to do for you?" Be specific and ask in the positive assurance that your prayers will be answered.

RESOURCES FOR FURTHER SCRIPTURE-JOURNALING

There are many fine books that can serve as an added resource in scripture study. In addition to devotional materials from The Upper Room, books of sermons, and biblical commentaries, you might try any of the following. Remember that these books are to serve as grist for the mill for journaling (not simply as something to be read informationally).

The Gospel in Solentiname by Ernesto Cardenal in 4 vols. (Orbis, 1982). The people of the church in Solentiname, Nicaragua, shared in a Gospel dialogue each Sunday in which they read a portion of scripture and then each shared their own insights on the Gospels. This Bible study-sharing is recorded in four books. The discussions are simple, earnest, and thought-provoking.

Jesus, Heaven on Earth (Orbis, 1980), *The Jesus Community* (Orbis, 1981), *The Jesus Option* (Orbis, 1982) by Joseph Donders. Written as reflections on the Gospels for the three cycles of the lectionary, these books may enable you to better apply the Gospels to your own life.

A Month with Christ: A Way to Pray the Gospels by J. Murray Elwood (Ave Maria Press, 1979). Elwood presents thirty scripture passages with response sections on "Christ in My Eyes," "Christ in My Heart," and "Christ in My Hands" to stimulate prayer. This book lends itself well to structured prayer-journaling.

NOTES

1. John Wesley, *The Works of the Reverend John Wesley,* Vol. V (Grand Rapids, MI: Zondervan Publishing House), p. 3.

2. Walter Wink, *Transforming Bible Study* (Nashville: Abindgon, 1980), pp. 82-83.

3. Parker Palmer, "Lectio Divina: Another Way to Learn," *Pendle Hill Newsletter,* Fall 1984, p. 1.

4. M. Robert Mulholland, Jr., *Shaped by the Word: The Power of Scripture in Spiritual Formation* (Nashville: The Upper Room, 1985), p. 54.

5. John Steinbeck, *The Winter of Our Discontent* (New York: Viking Press, 1961; New York: Bantam Books, 1961), p. 56.

JOURNALING IN RESPONSE TO SCRIPTURE

Three

Journaling with Guided Meditations

It was a Christmas pageant, but the familiar story was told with a modern slant. María and José were undocumented migrant workers, forced to leave a farm just before the birth of their first child. As they searched for a place to stay, the participants followed them in a parade.

Turned out by the farmer, they went to a hotel to ask for work. The proprietess suggested they try the local church. The priest there sent them on to the welfare office, where they were scathingly served red tape. In the plot of this pageant, José and María then turned to each other in tears, despairing. As they stood, hunched together in a hug, magical music filled the air. A small angel appeared to them and took them to their "manger": a parking lot bonfire staffed by bag ladies and winos who ended up as midwives and congratulators.

My daughter was the angel. In rehearsal, she was alternately a self-assured three-year-old and an unwilling draftee. She really wanted to play Mary. Up until the last minute, we were unsure whether she would be able to say her line or lead María and José to the appropriate place.

She was able to be part of the processional following the young parents-to-be up until the moment when she had to get her costume on. So she witnessed the plot unfolding at the farm and the hotel. She saw people she knew turning away Jesus' parents. And she began to cry. Her tears flowed from a broken heart. Didn't everyone know how to share? What was wrong with her friends (acting as farmer and hotel owner) that they would say "No room here" to Mary and Joseph? Would there be a place special enough for Jesus to be born?

My husband carried our sobbing daughter to where she quickly put on her angel costume—an old white pillowcase with armholes, cardboard wings covered with aluminum foil. Would she be able to present her key role in such a state?

José and María were spurned by the welfare worker. They embraced. Angel music sounded. And there she came, her face so full of life and light that those watching felt the tears stream down their faces. This young angel felt the importance of her role: Others had rejected the holy couple; she would lead them to a place to birth a king. The story was real to her even though, on another level, she knew it was just a play.

The reality with which this three-year-old angel felt the nativity story caused all of us to look again at the familiar. Christmas had become a nice, easy picture-book-pretty story. Yet it had been hard for Joseph and Mary. Had they felt rejection? Had they been afraid? Were there "good people" (friends?) who turned away from them when they were most in need? Did they feel the strength that came, ultimately, only from heaven?

Through an angel's eyes, we saw the grittiness of two young persons, surrounded by their own tensions and tears, searching for a place—anywhere—where they could quietly give birth to their firstborn. We felt the indignity of anyone daring to turn them away. We, too, were betrayed that nice people—people we knew, ourselves—had said

"No room" to Jesus' parents and continued to say no to countless others in the same position throughout the ages.

And we, too, were touched by the magic that only God could pull off: a simple stable, hay instead of quilts, animals instead of midwives, a savior born in an unexpected place. A miracle in that time and ours. We, too, heard the angel music and knew the innocence of the love that reached out to Joseph, Mary, and Jesus even as God reached out to us in that surprising birth. We felt the Christmas magic—through an angel's eyes.

Children offer the world a special blend of fantasy and reality. A preschooler can tell you that he is the father of two imaginary children even as he asks for details on his own birth and infancy. The nine-year-old may study the space program in science class and apply that information to fantasy play, with herself as Sally Ride. Children remind us that our "real" lives can be nurtured by our imaginations.

God gave humanity the twin gifts of reason and imagination. Both can be used to bring oneself closer to the creative Spirit. As we have grown into adulthood, many of us have felt more comfortable with the rational, the provable, what we understand. Yet we may find deep spiritual growth when we allow ourselves to explore the unknown and limitless possibilities of our imagination. As Morton Kelsey writes:

> Spiritual discovery, making a direct and creative encounter with spiritual reality, may well depend on developing one's imaginative capabilities. We have two hemispheres of the brain, one dealing with logic and language and the other with images, shapes, art, and story. If we are to be whole people we need to learn to use both sides of the brain and deal with our imaginative capacities. The images arising from the depths of us in dreams or fantasies or intuitions are one way by which we are brought into contact with the spiritual world. Without the use of images and imagination it is nearly impossible to obtain knowledge of the depth of ourselves or of the spiritual reality beyond us.[1]

The secular scientific world has also acknowledged the power of the imagination. O. Carl Simonton and Stephanie Matthews-Simonton use visualization techniques with cancer patients. Their studies show that the patients who learn to relax and develop positive attitudes through the practice of meditation have the best response to medical treatment of their disease.[2] Medical self-help books such as *The Well Body Book* encourage the use of an "imaginary doctor" and guided meditation as part of the healing process.[3]

The imaginative mind can be a powerful force in self-healing and moving toward the wholeness toward which God calls us. We can integrate reason and imagination, what is proven and what is unknown, our conscious and our subconscious thoughts. Guided meditations take us on a journey deep into our psyche where imagination plays with reality. On this journey, we can come in touch with the God who is at all levels of our consciousness.

This week you will experience guided meditation as an impetus for journaling. Each meditation has a scriptural base that can lead to your own spiritual discovery. Let yourself enter fully into each meditation, confident that you will feel God's presence. Guided meditation presents scripture in a new light. Whereas the previous chapter gave opportunity to come closer to the word of God in a cognitive way, this chapter offers a chance to know the Bible in an affective or emotional mode. Certainly we want to use both head and heart as we immerse ourselves in the word of God.

There are several ways you could experience the meditations as "guided" even though you will not have a leader reading out loud to you. Carolyn Stahl Bohler, writing as Carolyn Stahl in *Opening to God*, suggests:

> You could then read through the meditation several times, close your eyes, and do the meditation according to your memory. It does not need to be precise. Or, you may want to read the meditation into a tape recorder and play it back for

yourself. If you do this, be careful to read very slowly. Feel free to turn the tape machine off and on while you meditate, to give yourself whatever time you need before the next spoken words. Another method would be to read a small section of the meditation; close your eyes and experience that. Open your eyes and read the next phrase; close your eyes and experience that, and so on.[4]

In preparation for each day's meditation, read the scripture verse and any background notes. If you are using a tape-recorded meditation, make the recording ahead of time so you can experience the meditation fresh and new. Then find a comfortable position and sit as straight as possible with legs and arms uncrossed. Take several deep breaths or use other relaxation techniques so that you are most receptive to God's Spirit working within you during this time of meditation. Experience the meditation in whatever way feels best to you (see previous suggestions.) Do not try to force the experience, but keep in mind eight "Special Guidelines" suggested by Bohler:

(a) You may "see," but you may simply get a sense of the scene.
(b) Practice does increase your ability to image.
(c) No matter what happens in your imagery, that is OK.
(d) If you think "nothing" is happening, ask yourself what that "nothing" is.
(e) If you ever feel the need for assistance in your meditation, bring it into your imagery. You can bring in a helper, friend, or whatever you need.
(f) No matter what happens—"good" or "bad"—this is simply what is occurring now. It can and will change.
(g) Debrief or ground the experience after the meditation.
(h) Do not worry about succeeding, competing, or being appropriate. Simply let go and let the meditation move along as it will.[5]

There may be a meditation that touches you in a special way so that one day does not seem enough time. If you continue to think about images that arise from a particular meditation, you may want to spend more than one day journaling in response to it. Again, the goal here is not finishing the material but more importantly, coming closer to God through the practice of journaling.

The asterisks in each meditation are meant to be pausing points. At each asterisk, take some time to image what you have just read. If you are taping the meditation ahead of time, allow a period of silence after each asterisk. And remember that you have the freedom to turn the tape recorder off and on to give yourself needed time for meditation.

The meditations for this week will take you on a journey of faith that begins in the yes-saying of accepting Christ and then permeates all of life.

Day One: Responding to Jesus' Call
Day Two: Following Jesus
Day Three: Feeling the Power of God's Spirit
Day Four: Forgiving and Being Forgiven
Day Five: Receiving the Blessing of Jesus
Day Six: Discerning the Meaning of Jesus' Words
Day Seven: Sharing God's Message of Peace

Day One: Responding to Jesus' Call

Sit quietly and breathe deeply. When you feel relaxed and ready, experience the meditation.

You are a strong young man, and you are walking along a dusty country road with a group of comrades and your leader.

You are very strong, and you are very dark from the hot sun under which you made your living hauling in the teeming nets of fish from the Galilean sea.

You worked and you dreamed because you, like all your people, looked for the coming of the Anointed of God who would free your people from the oppressor's yoke and restore to them their place among the nations that they knew in David's time.*

One day your brother came to you excitedly and said that he had met a compelling man and urged you to come and see. You did, and you, too, found something in this man that made you leave your nets and follow him.

You were not alone in this rash act. Eleven others followed, too. And there was no regret. This man was different. He spoke, and the hushed crowds hung on his daring words. He touched the eyes of the blind, and they saw; the ears of the deaf, and they heard; the limbs of the lame, and they walked.*

Every day was filled with wonder and new life.

All of you were certain the Kingdom of God had come.

And then a shadow fell across your path. The leader set his face to Jerusalem.*

You followed behind him, hesitant and afraid. He walked on ahead, a lonely and strangely frightening figure.

And suddenly he turned and confronted all of you: "Who do men say that I am?" he asked.

Haltingly you repeated the rumors. "Some say you are John the Baptist." "Some say you are Elijah." "Some say one of the other prophets."

And then his sad, dark, all-seeing eyes fell on you. The voice struck deep chords in the depths of your spirit.

"Whom do you say that I am?"*

Let the ages fall away. Come back to this place, this time. You are you.

The eyes still hold you. The voice still questions.

"Who do you say I am?"*[6]

Scripture Reference: Mark 8:27-29.

Day Two: Following Jesus

Find a comfortable position and sit quietly with your eyes closed.* Take a few deep breaths, centering your body and soul on the Living Christ.*

We are going on a journey through time. Let yourself experience this journey as your own. We start out in the countryside of Judea. Picture yourself as a young woman among a large crowd of people gathered on a hillside to hear the new prophet, Jesus, speak. Seated under a gnarled old tree, surrounded by those called disciples, he looks out lovingly on this crowd. Then, in a voice that is gentle yet carries stronger than the wind, this Jesus begins to speak.

You strain forward to catch his words. It feels as if he is talking just to you alone. He speaks of how to find true happiness. You think of your life and what this teaching might mean to you. Am I meek? merciful? a peacemaker?* Your thoughts come back to what he is saying, catching a phrase about "your light must shine before people so they will see all the good things you do and praise God." The words settle deep within your soul. How can I, a woman, let my light shine?*

We move in time. Intrigued by his teachings, you have been following Jesus, quietly blending into the crowd that is almost always with him. You are coming to know the men and women who work most closely with Jesus. You are learning about servanthood from the women he called: Mary, Joanna, Susanna, and others. The question is still with you: How can I let my light shine? You are puzzled. Your society has made you feel less a person because of your femaleness. And now this Jesus is helping you see the God-image inside yourself. You have watched Jesus relate to women. There was one brave sister who reached out to touch the hem of his cloak. "Courage, my daughter! Your faith has made you well!" Another woman, a Canaanite, asked for her daughter's healing. "You are a woman of great faith. What you want will be done for you," Jesus said. He faces each woman as if she matters. How does this caring attitude mesh with what you have been brought up to believe about yourself?*

The years go by. You remained a faithful follower of Jesus, although you were always careful to remain anonymous in the crowd. Now you are full of sorrow. Three days ago you stood among a group of women at the foot of the cross on which Jesus was crucified. Mary Magdalene, Salome, Mary, and others watched and prayed as their beloved friend died a painful death. Remember how you felt as part of that group which silently supported him through the agony and pain.*

Now you are drawing water from a city well when you

hear familiar voices shouting at the top of their lungs. Can this be Mary Magdalene and Mary? How can they be so full of joy when Jesus is dead? You hear their breathless cries ringing throughout Jerusalem. "He is risen! Jesus is alive!" You wonder at the power of these women that they should be the first to see the resurrected Jesus.*

Travel through time to another time and place. You sit among Christian friends while a letter is read to you from the apostle Paul. He sends personal greetings to many who are gathered with you in the Roman church. As the letter is read, affirming each person's ministry, you watch the face of that person as their name is read. You see the faces of brothers Aquila, Epaenetus, Andronicus, and Rufus as they eagerly receive Paul's words. Your sisters are pleased to hear the apostle greet them personally, too: Phoebe, Priscilla, Mary, Junias, Tryphaena, Tryphosa, Rufus' mother, and Olympas. And when your name is read—"to Julia"—you think back to when you were so young, following Jesus cautiously at a distance. Now you are old. You work among those known openly as Christians. You see the results of your own ministry and sharing. You feel the empowerment which comes in knowing the risen Christ. And, as the letter from Paul is read at its conclusion, you bow your head in thanksgiving, echoing the apostle's words: "To the only God, who alone is all-wise, be glory through Jesus Christ forever!"*

Now, having journeyed through time and space, take a few moments to return to the present time and place, opening your eyes when ready.[7]

Scripture Reference: Matt. 5:1-16, 9:20-22, 15:21-28, 27:55-56, 28:1-10; Luke 8:1-3; Rom. 16:1-15, 27.

Day Three: Feeling the Power of God's Spirit

Close your eyes. Relax your neck and shoulders. After a minute or two of deep breathing, continue with this guided meditation.

Feel God's presence that comes to you in power and glory. The clouds swirl around you as you feel yourself transported through time and space to a valley. Look around you and see, to your horror, that the valley is filled with dry bones. What is the predominant color of the valley floor? How do you feel as your eyes survey the thousands of bones around you?*

You are glad that God is with you. Then God surprises you with this question: "Mortal, can these bones come back to life?" Your answer comes quickly, "Sovereign Lord, only you can answer that!" Look out at the valley of dry bones and consider again God's question: Is it possible that these bones might yet live?*

Then the Almighty's voice comes to you in authority: "Prophesy to the bones. Tell these dry bones to listen to the word of the Lord. Tell them that I, the Sovereign Lord, am saying to them: I am going to put breath into you and bring you back to life. I will give you sinews and muscles and cover you with skin. I will put breath into you and bring you back to life. Then you will know that I am the Lord."

Even as you survey the dry, dead piles of bones, you somehow believe these words and know that God's power can work even this miracle. Think of your people living in exile far away from their beloved Jerusalem. Consider the dryness of their lives, how lonely and disconnected many feel. Hear the familiar song:

> By the waters of Babylon,
> there we sat down and wept,
> when we remembered Zion.
> —Psalm 137:1

Take a few moments to visualize the faces of your brother and sister Israelites, especially those who feel their God has abandoned them. As they languish in the agony of exile, how are their lives like the dry bones?*

You know yourself to be a prophet, but the words rarely

come easily. Take a deep breath and prophesy as God told you to. Hear your words as they resound in your ears.* Then as you continue to share the good news of life from God, you hear a new sound. This sound is unlike any you have heard before; it is clickety, rattling, unearthly. Look around you to see where this strange sound comes from.*

Your eyes open wide as you see the dry bones coming to life as if operated by some hidden puppeteer. Bodies begin to take shape, bone and sinew and muscle and skin. But you realize that these bodies are devoid of life or breath.*

God's voice comes more tenderly this time. You listen, and then you feel the divine power swelling up within you as you prophesy to the wind as God has instructed.

"Wind, come from the east!
Come from the west!
Blow hither and thither from north and south.
Blow mightily into this place and then lovingly into
  each body here. Let your fresh air fill and
  bring to life these dead ones."

You stand waiting, and as your eyes expectantly search the skies, you feel the wind swirling around you and through the valley. In front of you, the bodies begin to sway, to stand, to dance with life. It seems there is a powerful army before you where recently only a pile of dry, dead bones lay.*

The work feels complete. Then the power comes again, intensely. God's voice rings in your ears: "The people of Israel are like these bones. In their minds, they are dried up, devoid of hope, no future available. You, my friend and my prophet, you tell them that I, the Sovereign, will open their graves. I will take them from their graves and return them to their homeland. Then they will know that I am God, the one who put my breath in them, brought them to life, and let them live in their own land. This is my promise. I have spoken."

Suddenly the voice is gone, the air is still. You look around the valley, thinking of the events and phrases of this incredible encounter with God. Your strength builds as you contemplate the messages still to be delivered to the people of Israel.*

While the power of God's spirit blowing breath into dry bones is still with you, prepare yourself to return to your contemporary situation. Where in your world do you see dryness and death? Visualize the spirit of God blowing in and through any areas of your life that seem dry and lifeless. Be assured that God's power can transform even the bleakest moment or situation.* When you are ready, return to the present and open your eyes.

Scripture Reference: Ezek. 37:1-15.

Day Four: Forgiving and Being Forgiven

> Take a few deep breaths to relax and center in.... Now get a sense of yourself inside a beautiful temple or sacred place.* ... Notice the structure, the colors, the fragrances, and the people who are there.... Allow yourself to absorb the beauty, the dignity, the sense of majesty.*... Now become aware that you have a gift in your hand.... Walk up toward the altar and place the gift upon the altar. While you are there, standing or kneeling, think back to see if there is anyone toward whom you feel anger or resentment or who you think holds anger toward you.... Become aware of that anger within you, that resentment, or that unfinished business, whatever it may be.*... Now walk back down the aisle of the temple or sacred place to go to talk to that person whom you have not forgiven or with whom you do not have peace. ... Encounter that person and communicate with that person in any way that seems most effective.... You can always ask for assistance, if needed, in order to communicate with that person.*... When you feel ready, go back with your gift to the sacred place or temple and to the altar.... Again, reflect to see if there is anyone with whom you have unfinished

business. . . . If so, then go out again, find that person and communicate with him or her.*. . . Again, go back into the temple and up to the altar with your gift. Become aware again of the majesty within this place and the sense of cleansing forgiveness. Sense God's all pervading love moving through you. Offer your gift at the altar and experience its being accepted.* When you feel ready, move out of the temple and into your daily life. . . . When you are ready, open your eyes.[8]

Scripture Reference: Matt. 5:23-24.

Day Five: Receiving the Blessing of Jesus[9]

In ancient Jewish society, "any flow of blood rendered the bleeder ritually unclean, and to be unclean was to be untouchable, along with lepers and cadavers. . . . All of the women within in Judaism of Jesus' day were periodically unclean by virtue of menstruation."[10]

Listen to one such "unclean" woman speak to you; let her story become your own.

"It's hard for me even to say what I was. The shame I felt for twelve years threatens to overwhelm me once again even as I dare to say to you that I was 'the woman who never stopped menstruating.' What began as a physical ailment turned into a label, a plague, a state of ostracism. I was *unclean*. Unacceptable. Unloved.

"At first, I fought against the ailment. I tried doctor after doctor. I listened to anyone who thought they might have an answer to my problem, even tried 'cures' that sounded improbable or crazy or dangerous. I would have done anything to regain my health. Can you imagine the energy that drained daily from my soul even as the blood left my body in a never-ending flow? Have you ever had others look at you in disgust for something you couldn't help? Have there been times when you, too, were the victim of mean jests and harsh words?*

71

"After a time, even my friends drifted away. Their well-meant advice often pierced my soul. 'What sin have you committed to deserve all this suffering? Why don't you just ask God to forgive you? You're just being stubborn.' When the bleeding persisted and persisted, despite all the remedies I tried and advice I suffered, people decided there was something terribly wrong with me, and I was left without a friend.

"There came a time when it seemed clear even to me that no one could help me. I tried to resign myself to the fact that I would bleed forever, not enough to die physically, but enough to make me die slowly inside. I was dying of loneliness, of lack of love, of the absence of hope. I realized I'd always been alone, unloved, hopeless. I wondered why I should even go on living, for certainly life meant little to me.

"You can't imagine how much I longed for the touch of a human hand. Even the children on the street knew not to come near me. Twelve years without a friendly hand on my shoulder, a hug from a friend, a kiss from a husband, a squirmy child on my lap. Twelve long years.*

"And so there I was, my emotional and physical resources exhausted. There seemed little reason to go on. Then (and I thank God for this day!) I was on my way to market when I overheard a conversation about Jesus. 'A new faith healer!' someone said. 'He can heal the blind, lame, and deaf!' another woman said. I didn't dare stop to ask them details, but I kept my ears open for Jesus' name. Little by little, I picked up bits and pieces of conversation that convinced me I had to see this Jesus for myself.

"And then, on that incredible day when I saw him, it came to me that if I could only touch the hem of his garment, I might be healed. It was a risk, of course. The man was a rabbi. He would certainly be outraged at being touched by an unclean woman (for that would make him unclean as well). But if I could just sneak up and lightly touch the part of his cloak that drags in the dust, he wouldn't even know. Perhaps I could receive some of his power without causing a scene.

"I've never been so afraid in all my life. But as soon as I touched his hem, I knew I was cured. The wet stickiness was gone; new energy poured through my body. But before I could even thank God for this gift, Jesus stopped short, turned around, and asked 'Who touched my clothes?' I was horrified. I couldn't face having him condemn me for my audacious behavior.

"So I fell to the ground in front of him. I couldn't bear to see his eyes or the eyes of the crowd upon me. I poured out the story of my life. I asked for his forgiveness. I lay there in the dust waiting for his anger, the venom that this man had a right to bestow upon an unclean woman. I lay there and waited. But it didn't come.

"And can you believe it? He looked at me with gentleness and compassion. 'Daughter, your faith has made you well; go in peace, and be healed of your disease.'

"When he blessed me with those words, I jumped up and ran through the streets, joyfully announcing my healing. It didn't matter if I bumped into someone. I was free to make new friends, to touch, to hold, to share love. All because I dared to touch that man of power!

"Hear my story. Feel both my earlier shame and the unending joy I now experience from life. And receive the blessing of Jesus who says to you, as he said to me, 'Be free!' "*

Scripture Reference: Mark 5:25-34.

Day Six: Discerning the Meaning of Jesus' Words

Shrug your shoulders up and down five times. Let your head hang heavy to the front, right side, back, then left side. Breathe deeply to prepare yourself for the meditation.

Picture yourself living long ago in Judea. You have heard about one Jesus of Nazareth who heals the sick, teaches about God, challenges authority. One day you decide to join the crowds following Jesus. You listen carefully to his words, and when a young man comes to Jesus with a question, you observe the interaction with interest.

"Teacher, what good thing must I do to receive eternal life?" You, too, would like to know. You are puzzled by Jesus' tone of voice when he responds, "Why do you ask me concerning what is good? There is only One who is good. Keep the commandments if you want to enter life."

The young man pushes for specificity. "What commandments?"

You see Jesus look at the young man carefully.

"Do not commit murder; do not commit adultery; do not steal; do not accuse anyone falsely; respect your father and your mother; and love your neighbor as yourself."

You think over these commandments, knowing their importance.* Then your reverie is interrupted by the young man's persistence: "I have obeyed all these commandments. What else do I need to do?" You listen carefully, wondering what the questioner wants to hear.

Jesus speaks softly: "If you want to be perfect, go and sell all you have and give the money to the poor, and you will have riches in heaven; then come and follow me."

A strange look crosses the young man's face. He gazes down at the ground, shakes his head, then slowly turns away, his shoulders hunched in dejection.*

You are still thinking of the sadness in the young seeker's eyes as Jesus and his disciples continue in conversation. Jesus speaks words of stone: "I assure you: it will be very hard for rich people to enter the kingdom of heaven. I repeat: it is much harder for a rich person to enter the kingdom of God than for a camel to go through the eye of a needle."

Your eyes open wide—did you hear him right? What can these words mean?*

You are not alone in your puzzlement. Jesus' friends push him to explain. "Who, then, can be saved?"

Jesus looks straight at his friends and answers, "This may seem impossible for human beings, but for God, everything is possible." The conversation continues. Your thoughts are darting here and there as you try to discern what these words might mean for you.* What possible things is God ready to do in your life?* Do you understand yourself as rich or poor?

When you are ready, imagine yourself walking away from Jesus and his followers. Journey down a eucalyptus-lined road, then reenter the present when ready.

Scripture Reference: Matt. 19:16-26.

Day Seven: Sharing God's Message of Peace

Close your eyes and imagine yourself in a spaceship orbiting planet Earth. See the outline of the various continents as you slowly circle the planet. Note to yourself some of the landmarks familiar to you: oceans, countries, cities, mountain ranges.*

Now the spaceship is preparing to land. The air becomes fuzzy, and you cannot tell in what direction your ship is going. You feel the gentle impact as the ship meets the water. As the air clears, you see that the waves are washing you toward land. You wonder where you are. Will this be a familiar place?

When your spaceship has come ashore, you see that the sandy beach parallels a range of mountains. One peak in particular stands high and majestic in front of you; you begin to walk toward its summit. The trail is not hard, and you enjoy the vegetation along the way. You are amazed at how effortless your hike is. Soon you are almost at the top; and there, carved into the side of the mountain peak, is a grassy meadow in which you see signs of life.*

You stand in amazement, for the living creatures gathered here are diverse: lions, cows, bears, sheep, wolves, people, snakes. The sound of children's laughter fills the air, as does the fragrance of violets and honeysuckle. As you approach, all the creatures stop their activity and turn toward you. You do not feel threatened but, rather, invited to join their company.*

As you spend time in this strange and wonderful place, you begin to sense the holiness of this hill. You feel a bit more holy yourself and have trouble imagining the world as you have known it. This unusual place, with its mixed menagerie, seems the norm. A world where violence exists doesn't make sense. You try to think only of this holy hill and its brilliant light and peace, but something inside you keeps returning to the world you have just left—a world where wolves and sheep do not live together in peace, a world where children must be protected from many kinds of harm.*

It becomes clear to you that you have been brought to this peaceful mountain for a purpose. Your experience of this holy hill prods you to share this vision of peace. So, even though it is hard for you to think of leaving, you say goodbye to this company and return to your spaceship. Catapulting back into the starry skies, you think again of the world you know. Particular places come to mind. You think of the places most familiar to you—cities where you and your friends live in your own country. You focus on places that are only names on the map, some of whose inhabitants are considered enemies of your country. You realize how enormous planet Earth is and how diverse its people.*

You are thankful that your message is one that can apply to anyone in any place or situation. You feel strengthened by the time you spent on the holy hill.

Choose a place, any place, and land your spaceship so you can visit the people who live there. See those people before you. How do they dress? What sort of homes do they live in?* Approach an individual or group with confidence, and share of your experience on the holy hill. Give your message of peace, knowing it will be accepted. Remember the wolf and sheep next to one another, the child playing near a poisonous snake, and know that even these people can become a community with all others in the world.*

When you feel that these people understand, move on to another place. Move and share your message as many times as you want. Realize that people everywhere are hungering for your message: the assurance that peace is indeed possible. Feel connected to all humanity as you share in God's peace.*

When it feels right, return to the present time, still carrying the sense of God's possibility and your own power as a peacemaker.

Scripture Reference: Is. 11:6-9; Matt. 5:9.

RESOURCES FOR FURTHER JOURNALING WITH GUIDED MEDITATIONS

Certain books specifically offer a collection of guided meditations for group or individual use. Among these you might want to try:

Opening to God by Carolyn Stahl (The Upper Room, 1977) is an excellent resource on "imagery meditation" and its use. Among the thirty meditations included in this book is one used above: "Forgiving and Being Forgiven."

The Other Side of Silence: A Guide to Christian Meditation by Morton Kelsey (Paulist Press, 1976) gives extensive background on meditation, then offers seventy pages of biblical reflections, stories, and poems that lend themselves to journaling use.

The following books, though not written specifically as meditations, by their nature become windows to the soul when used in journaling.

A Certain Life: Contemporary Meditations on the Way of Christ by Herbert O'Driscoll (Seabury Press, 1980) guides the

reader through the life and time of Jesus in forty meditations that can be especially meaningful as a Lenten discipline of journaling.

O'Driscoll's *Portrait of a Woman: Meditations on the Mother
of Our Lord* (Seabury Press, 1981) and *Crossroads: Times of
Decision for People of God* (Seabury Press, 1982) explore
further dimensions of the human soul in Mary's life story
and that of fifteen more of God's people (from Noah to
Bishop Oscar Romero).

Ragman and Other Cries of Faith by Walter Wangerin, Jr.
(Harper and Row, 1984) shares intensely beautiful and poign-
ant contemporary stories that relate to the Christian faith
and understanding of the world.

NOTES

1. Morton Kelsey, *Adventure Inward: Christian Growth through Personal
Journal Writing* (Minneapolis: Augsburg, 1980), pp. 141-142.

2. O. Carl Simonton and Stephanie Matthews-Simonton, as described
by Kenneth R. Pelletier, *Mind as Healer, Mind as Slayer: A Holistic
Approach to Preventing Stress Disorders* (New York: Dell, 1977), pp.
252-262.

3. Michael Samuels and Hal Bennett, *Well Body Book* (New York: Random House, 1973), pp. 8-14.

4. Carolyn Stahl, *Opening to God* (Nashville: The Upper Room, 1977),
pp. 32-33.

5. Ibid., p. 50.

6. Verna Dozier, "Responding to the Call to Ministry," *Action Informa-
tion*, April 1980, pp. 4-5.

7. This meditation was originally published in *Women: Called to Ministry*,
a study guide by Anne Broyles and Margaret A. Turbyfill (Nashville:
Division of Ordained Ministry, The United Methodist Church, 1985),
pp. 8-9.

8. Stahl, pp. 65-66.

9. This meditation is adapted from Mallonee Hubbard's article, "The Woman Who Never Stopped Menstruating," *Daughters of Sarah,* November/December 1985, pp. 8-10.

10. Hubbard, p. 8.

JOURNALING WITH GUIDED MEDITATIONS

Four

Journaling from Dreams

She heard a vague buzzing. Deep in sleep, she tried to ignore the alarm clock insistently calling to her. She reached over and turned it off, pulled the covers over her head, and tried to go back to sleep. "This dream is so good," she thought, "I don't want to lose it." A garbage truck noisily pulled up in front of her apartment building; her sleep was disturbed by the clanging of cans and the whirr of the truck's motor. She gave up on sleep, sat up in bed, and tried to remember what the dream had been about.

Details of the dream were fuzzy in her mind, but she knew the dream had been comforting. The other person in the dream—it didn't seem like anyone she actually knew—had made her feel special, cared for, safe. This person seemed to have characteristics of several people she knew, but she couldn't place her finger on who it was.

Throughout the day, she remembered bits and pieces of the dream. It was like piecing together a quilt or putting the puzzle pieces into place. The dream might not sound important to anyone else or have meaning for another person, but certain aspects of her life began to make sense in a new way.

All persons dream. Yet the majority of our sleep-dreaming is lost to us. Unless we have a particularly frightening nightmare or happen to be involved in a vivid dream upon waking, the hours of sleep when our unconscious mind is involved in dreaming are not brought to conscious thought.

Yet dreams are a special gift of our sleeping hours. Through these subconscious experiences, we can sometimes find needed meaning when we awake. Suggesting that dreams "carry the seed-nature of a person," Ira Progoff writes: "Dreams are unselfconscious reflectors that express all the various levels of the individual psyche as it is in movement. Dreams express the outward circumstances of a person's life, his current problems and fears, and also the hopes and goals toward which he is consciously planning. In addition, however, dreams reflect the deeper-than-conscious goals that are seeking to unfold in a person's life."[1]

Those who use their dreams in journaling often discover those deeper meanings and levels that are present in dreams. The simple process of writing down our dreams gives us the opportunity to get in touch with a deep part of ourselves, what Alan McGlashan calls the "dreamer within."

Who is the "dreamer within"? In *Dreams: God's Forgotten Language*, John Sanford says: "We can look at it this way: if dreams have a meaning, it is clear that this meaning does not come from our conscious personality. And if we do not consciously make up our dreams out of our ego, out of that 'I' part of us with which we are familiar, then the meaning of our dreams comes from an unconscious source of our psychic life."[2]

Later in his book, Sanford details "dreams and visions in the Bible." From the multitude of examples of ordinary persons receiving extraordinary communication from the Creator through dreams and/or visions, it is clear that in both Old and New Testaments, dreams and visions were regarded as revelations from God. Dreams were simply another form of communication between God and humanity.[3] God's spirit can be the "dreamer within" who guides us closer to both our inner self and the One who created us.

Until we consciously and systematically record our dreams, many of us cannot fully experience the "dreamer within." Our dreams are separate from us, unavailable. But for those seeking a closer relationship to God, dreams may be an important link.

If Yahweh spoke to Abram, Jacob, Samuel, Daniel, Mary, Joseph, Peter, and Paul through their dreams, is it not possible that God is even now speaking to you in your dreams? "As our spiritual friends, our dreams are constantly encouraging us to be open to a fresh word from God— sometimes a word of reassurance, at other times of warning, guidance, or command. Whatever they say to us, our dreams can render God's presence so vividly that our lives will never be the same."[4]

Dreams are friends that come to us from God. Like all friends, dreams must be welcomed into our consciousness. How can you open yourself to receive the gifts of dreams? First, you can realize that dreams come to help, not to harm you. As you know that all aspects of your life come from God, affirm that dreams (even those with messages that may seem difficult or disturbing) can lead to closeness with God the Dreamer. Once you feel dreams as a positive and instrinsic force in your conscious and unconscious life, you can ready yourself to receive the dream-gifts.

Before going to sleep, pray for receptivity to God's messages that might come through any dream. You can prepare yourself to remember the dream(s) by placing either paper, pen, and flashlight or a small tape recorder next to the bed. When you awaken (in the middle of the night or in the morning), immediately record any bits and pieces of dreams that come to mind. Write or speak quickly, noting any details or feelings that come to your consciousness, even if they seem trivial or do not make sense to you at the time of recording.

The more you try to remember your dreams, the more easily these unconscious memories will come to the forefront of your mind. As you try to remember dreams of a specific time of sleep, other dreams may come back to you as well—dreams of childhood, recurring dreams, nightmares, fragments of dreams of long ago. Write down these remembrances, too.

Record dreams as you experience them. At this point, do not judge or censor or analyze. Rather than imposing your critical conscious mind upon the dream experience, let the dream rest safely for a time in the pages of your journal.

Upon rereading the dream as it is recorded in your journal, you may receive an important insight as to what a certain action signifies or who a character in the dream might represent. Such "figuring out" is fine if it comes easily. Otherwise, let the dreams gather in your journal; accumulate a "moving picture" of your own dream life.[5] Over a period of time you may be able to see certain patterns to your dreaming.

Without psychoanalyzing every portion of our dreams, we can often gain new insights into our spiritual journey by taking our written-down dreams and prayerfully considering what God might be saying to us in them. Dream analysis is rewarding and meaningful. Most of us can figure out certain meanings to our dreams but are not ready to give Freudian or Jungian connotations to our night-gifts. If you want to go into a deeper analysis of your dreams, you might wish to do further reading (see Resources for Further Journaling from Dreams) or take a course on dream analysis.

Be realistic about your own readiness and capability for deep dream analysis, however, and realize that one dream may be interpreted many ways. For instance, you might have a vivid dream about boxes. The box being an archetypal image in psychological analysis, you might conclude that you were feeling boxed in, ready to break out of the box or needing the security of a box. If you happened to be in the process of moving, however, the box dream might just reflect your literal situation of being surrounded by boxes![6]

This week your journaling will focus on dreams as a gift

from God to you and to your spirit-journey. Each night, try the process outlined above to open yourself and receive the gifts that might come from God in your dreams. In the daytime, you might want to reread the dream and fill in any further details. Ask yourself any of the following questions, as fits the nature of the dream:
• Am I actor or spectator in this dream?
• Who are the characters of the dream?
• How did I feel upon awaking?
• How do I feel now as I reread this dream?
• Is there anything familiar about this dream?
• Do any obvious meanings or messages jump out at me?

If there are nights when it is impossible for you to capture any fragments of dreaming, use your journaling time for jotting down bits and pieces of previous dreams that have remained in your mind for a long time. The questions above may apply to dreams of an earlier time as well.

Journaling dreams may become a daily discipline for you as you seek union with God's spirit in Christ. More likely, your journaling will take many different forms and you will journal about a particular dream when you need to work more with its meanings or when it has affected your heart and soul. However you use dreams in your journal, God the Dreamer will continue to speak to you in soft, subtle tones through the scenes that play out in your subconscious as you sleep.

God the Dreamer may also speak to us in our daydreams, guiding us to vision and then to live out our lives as they are meant to be. Daydreams, like their nightly counterparts, come from deep within, from God who is revealed to us in yet another way. So rather than passing off your daydream as "nonsense" or a waste of time, you may want to record a particular daydream in your journal for further consideration. Think of it as a "futuring" connection with God.

Whether a dream comes by day or night, greet it warmly as a friend, a message from God to a beloved child of God.

RESOURCES FOR FURTHER JOURNALING FROM DREAMS

Dreams: A Way to Listen to God by Morton Kelsey (Paulist Press, 1978).

Dreams: God's Forgotten Language by John A. Sanford (Crossroad, 1982).

Jung and the Bible by Wayne G. Rollins (John Knox Press, 1983).

Man and His Symbols by Carl G. Jung (Doubleday, 1969).

"Seventeen Suggestions for Interpreting Your Dreams," in *Adventure Inward* by Morton Kelsey (Augsburg, 1980).

The Interpretation of Dreams by Sigmund Freud (Modern Library, 1950).

"Working with Our Dreams," in *At a Journal Workshop* by Ira Progoff (Dialogue House Library, 1977), pp. 228-52.

NOTES

1. Ira Progoff, *At a Journal Workshop* (Dialogue House Library, 1977), p. 229.

2. John Sanford, *Dreams: God's Forgotten Language* (New York: Crossroad, 1982), p. 21.

3. Ibid., p. 116.

4. Leroy T. Howe, "Dreams as Spiritual Friends," *Weavings*, July/August 1987, p. 39.

5. Progoff, p. 231

6. Fran Cooper, in conversation with the author

JOURNALING FROM DREAMS

Five

Journaling in Response to Reading

The television show "Reading Rainbow" reminds its young viewer/readers that they can experience great and wondrous adventures through the pages of a book. New worlds can be visited, ideas formed, and preconceptions challenged as the reader enters into a fictional world. Reading, rather than being an escape from life, can increase one's capability to cope with the realities of life.

Some people concentrate their reading time on fiction; others prefer biography, scientific studies, or philosophy. Others read the daily newspaper and monthly magazines. Whatever our reading material, our daily times of reading can be the basis for dialogue between ourselves and God. As we read newspapers, magazines, or books, do certain phrases and quotations jump out at us? Are we gifted with a new idea or challenged to reconsider long-held beliefs?

Reading the daily paper can, in conjunction with journaling, be a conscious time of prayer for the world. We may write of our concern for earthquake victims, our fear of nuclear disaster, our joy at a new birth or a peace accord. As we journal in response to the daily news, we interact with what is happening in the world; we feel more strongly the connections between ourselves and others around the globe.

Magazine articles provide a seedbed for learning. Combined with journaling, these articles can lead us further. How is God being made manifest in research into the cause of AIDS? In the discussion about surrogate mothers? In the story of a young athlete killed by cocaine? How is our faith tested or strengthened by the topics of the articles we read? What belief systems make us react sharply in a positive or negative way to a certain author's point of view?

Books can educate, inspire, involve, transport us to another world. Why does a particular line from *Iacocca: An Autobiography* keep us thinking? How would we like to be like Winnie Mandela? Why do we feel so challenged by the young Polish priest in *City of Joy*? What do we learn of our society through *Habits of the Heart*? How is our theology expanded by reading *Medicine Woman*?

Our daily reading, whether inspirational or business-related, nonfiction or fantasy, can provide a fertile ground for discovering the God within us as we interact with the passages that strike us most keenly as we read.

Not everything we read will provide the impetus for journaling. But the more we allow ourselves to respond to what our reading elicits from us, the more often our minds and hearts will make the connection between what is on the written page and what we ourselves need to write as dialogue with God. Obviously, certain types of reading material are more likely to encourage us to make God-connections than others. *Guideposts*, *The Upper Room*, religious novels, and *The Christian Science Monitor* will necessarily make us think of God and God's role in our world. *People*, *Tiger Beat Star*, and *TV Guide* are unlikely to provide thought-provoking material about life's important issues. But each person needs a variety of reading sources in order to best understand the world in which we have been placed as God's people.

As you read, it will be helpful to keep a pen or marker

handy for underlining those words and phrases that leap out at you, asking for further examination. The moment of reading may not be the time for journaling. But an important sentence underlined as you read the newspaper on the ous to work can be the grist for that evening's journaling experience. Or a page turned down in a novel might be a reminder that you want to work more with the idea expressed in the third paragraph.

You will want to reread the words you have marked, giving time for deeper meanings to sink into your consciousness. You might do this at the beginning of your journaling time after some centering (deep breathing, relaxation, prayer). Let yourself ease into further examination of the quote. How do these words challenge or perturb or comfort you? What might you learn of God in this passage? What are you discovering about yourself in your choice of this section of reading?

It may not feel immediately natural to go into such detail about a sentence or paragraph or even the summary of a longer article. Certainly, not every quote will lend itself to this process. But the more you take the time to focus on the words that have grabbed your attention, the easier this process will become. Unless you use one of the books described later in this chapter that offer a daily quote, journaling in response to quotes will probably be an occasional addition to your regular journaling. Remember that journaling is a freeing discipline of the spirit. Some days you will need to journal about a particular event of that day; other days your journaling may focus on scripture or a non-scriptural passage or a dream.

For the next week you will use one quotation for each day's journaling. Questions are suggested as a starting point to respond to these quotes, but you should in no way feel limited to these beginning points of thought. If during this week you are challenged by particular words in your own reading, use your own quote for journaling rather than or in addition to the quotation provided.

Each day, center into your journaling time. Read the quotation. Reread it. Then prayerfully consider the questions given and journal your responses.

God comes to us in many ways. May this week of journaling in response to quotations bring you ever closer to the Lover of the World who has gifted us with the word and with words.

Day One

> Mama: "There is always something left to love. And if you ain't learned that, you ain't learned nothing. . . . Child, when do you think is the time to love somebody the most; when they done good and made things easy for everybody? Well, then, you ain't through learning—because that ain't the time at all. It's when he's at his lowest and can't believe in hisself 'cause the world done whipped him so. When you starts measuring somebody, measure him right, child, measure him right. Make sure you done taken into account what hills and valleys he come through before he got to wherever he is."
> —Lorraine Hansberry,
> *A Raisin in the Sun*

What have been some of your hills and valleys?

How might these words from Isaiah 40:4-5 (KJV) speak to your hill or valley experience?

> Every valley shall be exalted, and every mountain and hill shall be made low: and the crooked shall be made straight, and the rough places plain.

Do particular persons come to mind as those who have experienced hills and valleys that you need to take into account as you relate to them? Write a prayer for these persons and your relationship to them.

Day Two

Do you not see how everything that happens keeps on being
a beginning?
And could it not be God's beginning since beginning is
always in itself so beautiful?

—Rainer Maria Rilke

Can you remember an experience of starting over again
and feeling the grace of a fresh beginning?
At this point, what do you see as God's new beginning
for you?
How do these Bible passages influence your thinking on
beginnings?
• Genesis 1:1-2
• John 1:1-5
• 2 Thessalonians 2:13

Day Three

Experiencing the present purely is being emptied and hollow; you catch grace as a [person] fills [a] cup under a
waterfall.

—Annie Dillard

In what ways do you "experience the present purely?"
Is the image of "being emptied and hollow" helpful to
your spiritual life? Can you perceive God's grace coming to
you as powerfully and simply as a waterfall?

Day Four

It does one good to feel that one has still a brother, who lives
and walks on this earth; when one has so many things to
think of, and many things to do, one sometimes gets the
feeling: Where am I? What am I doing? Where am I going?

—and one's brain reels, but then such a well-known voice as yours, or rather a well-known handwriting, makes one feel again firm ground under one's feet.

—Vincent Van Gogh

Who have been those brothers or sisters who have made you "feel again firm ground" under your feet?

Do you have Christian friends who share your spirit journey and support you as you figure out "Where am I? What am I doing? Where am I going?"

How are you such a friend to other seeking Christians?

Day Five

Look on the rising sun; there God does live,
    And gives his light and gives his heat away;
And flowers and trees and beasts and men receive
    Comfort in morning, joy in the noon day.
And we are put on Earth a little space,
    That we may learn to bear the beams of love.

—William Blake

How have you felt "comfort in morning, joy in the noon day?"

In your own life, how are you learning "to bear the beams of love"? When have you felt yourself a channel for God's love flowing through you to other people?

Day Six

To live is to be slowly born.
—Antoine de Saint-Exupéry

From the beginning till now the entire creation, as we know, has been groaning in one great act of giving birth; and not only creation, but all of us who possess the first-fruits of the Spirit, we too groan inwardly as we wait for our bodies to be set free.

—Romans 8:22-23 (JB)

Each of us experiences birth pangs. Some of us may actually experience childbirth. An important project or idea may be born through "pangs of birth." A new self may be the result of long laboring.

What has been your most life-changing birth experience?

How did you feel as you were giving birth?

Day Seven

> I think one must do the thing—whatever it is (and it changes from time to time)—that unites you to the flowing stream of the world. At any price, one must do it first. Otherwise one can do nothing, nothing at all. One is out of touch, out of grace.
>
> —Anne Morrow Lindbergh

What actions have you taken that have united you to "the flowing stream of the world"?

Have you felt the price of such actions?

How do Lindbergh's words connect to these words from James 2:14 (AP): "What good is it if one claims to have faith if one's actions do not prove it?"

RESOURCES FOR FURTHER JOURNALING WITH QUOTATIONS

The Martyred Christian by Dietrich Bonhoeffer, edited by Joan Winmill Brown (Macmillan, 1985) gives 160 readings from the works of the young German theologian who was executed by the Nazis for his participation in a plot to assassinate Hitler.

Through the Year with Wesley, edited by Frederick C. Gill (The Upper Room, 1983), shares a selection of the founder of Methodism's "living thoughts and pithy sayings, arranged for daily use."

The Dorothy Day Book: A Selection from Her Writings and Readings, edited by Margaret Garvey and Michael Garvey

(Templegate Publishers, 1982), offers 124 pages of short writings that challenge Christians and give insight into the cofounder of the Catholic Worker movement.

The Centering Moment and *Meditations of the Heart* by Howard Thurman (Friends United Press, 1980 and 1976) each contain short meditation-prayers by this poetic and pastoral black theologian.

The Healing Fountain: Writings Selected from Contemporary Christians, edited by Betty Thompson (Education and Cultivation Division, Board of Global Ministries, United Methodist Church, 1973), offers categorized selections of Christian writings with questions and suggestions for further journaling or group work.

Peacemaking: Day by Day (Pax Christi USA, 348 E. 10th, Erie, PA 16503) gives encouragement for peacemaking through daily selections of Bible passages, quotations, and short stories accompanied by lovely pen-and-ink drawings.

JOURNALING IN RESPONSE TO READING

Six

Journaling Conversations
or Dialogues

Roaming through London's streets and alleys one night, a nineteen-year-old found a ragged, terrified little girl. When Fynn took Anna home to his mother to care for her, there began a tender and beautiful relationship between the young man and the six-year-old theologian—a relationship he details in *Mister God, This Is Anna*. Their conversations taught him much about the universe and God and the meaning of life. Listen to this odd pair as they discuss the subject of God's love:

"Mister God made everything, didn't he?"

There was no point in saying I really didn't know. I said, "Yes."

"Even the dirt and the stars and the animals and the people and the trees and everything, and the pollywogs?" The pollywogs were those little creatures we had seen under the microscope.

I said, "Yes, he made everything."

She nodded her agreement. "Does Mister God love us truly?"

"Sure thing," I said. "Mister God loves everything."

"Oh," she said. "Well then, why does he let things get hurt and dead?" Her voice sounded as if she felt she had betrayed a sacred trust, but the question had been thought and it had to be spoken.

"I don't know," I replied. "There's a great many things about Mister God that we don't know about."

"Well then," she continued, "if we don't know many things about Mister God, how do we know he loves us?"

I could see that this was going to be one of those times, but thank goodness she didn't expect an answer to her question for she hurried on: "Them pollywogs, I could love them till I bust, but they wouldn't know, would they? I'm million times bigger than they are and Mister God is million times bigger than me, so how do I know what Mister God does?"

She was silent for a little while. Later I thought that at this moment she was taking her last look at babyhood. Then she went on:

"Fynn, Mister God doesn't love us." She hesitated. "He doesn't really, you know, only people can love. I love Bossy, but Bossy don't love me. I love the pollywogs, but they don't love me. I love you, Fynn, and you love me, don't you?"

I tightened my arm around her.

"You love me because you are people. I love Mister God truly, but he don't love me."

It sounded to me like a death-knell. "Damn and blast," I thought. "Why does this have to happen to people? Now she's lost everything." But I was wrong. She had got both feet planted firmly on the next stepping-stone.

"No," she went on, "no, he don't love me, not like you do, it's different, it's millions of times bigger."

I must have made some movement or noise for she levered herself upright and sat on her haunches and giggled. Then she launched herself at me and undid my little pang of hurt, cut out the useless spark of jealousy with the delicate sureness of a surgeon.

"Fynn, you can love better than any people that ever was, and so can I, can't I? But Mister God is different. You see, Fynn, people can only love outside and can only kiss outside, but Mister God can love you right inside, and Mister God can kiss you right inside, so it's different. Mister God ain't like us; we are a little bit like Mister God, but not much yet."[1]

The dialogue between Anna and Fynn not only raised important questions about God, love, and suffering. Their conversation enabled Anna to work through questions of faith. Fynn received new insight from and with her. Each of them was drawn closer to "Mister God" because they were able to share words and ideas in conversation.

Unless we are in a time of solitude or silence, we engage in dozens of conversations each day. Whether we are talking with family, friends, business acquaintances, or strangers, God may speak to us through a seemingly ordinary conversation. A short talk with the tree-trimmer or grocery clerk may spark a new idea. A long conversation with a trusted friend may influence the way we view ourselves and our world.

Recording our conversations gives us a chance to look at what we said, heard, and felt during them. What would we like to have said? Were there things we wish our conversation-partner had said? What meanings did we infer from specific words or phrases? Often the practice of writing our conversations gives us the opportunity to reflect on how God may use our own and others' words to proclaim God's greatness and mercy.

Not every conversation will necessarily be journal material. So relax! Do not engage in conversation with the thought of remembering specific words or phrases so you can write them down later. If you live with the openness that God may be speaking to you through your conversations (just as the Creator is speaking through dreams and readings and daily experience), then certain conversations may be valuable material for your journal.

Let your conversations flow naturally. If something in particular strikes you, make a mental note of it. But continue to concentrate on what the other person is saying, listening as actively as possible so that your relationship with that person (temporary or permanent) may be as meaningful as possible. Quaker George Fox spoke of "that of God in everyone." In your conversations, try to be open to "that of God" in another's words.

You do not need to try to quote exact conversations; what is important is to remember the general tone and feeling level. For example, a discussion with a neighbor who feels very differently from you on nuclear arms may cause you to journal the conversation, hoping to continue a loving dialogue later. Or a talk with your spouse may trigger the desire to record your words as a reminder of this particular stage of your marriage.

Journaling your conversations connects nicely to recording other daily events. The words you speak and hear are part of your everyday experience. The more you can develop the knack for writing down conversations as accurately as possible, the better you can record the details of your life.

A conversation need not be long or earthshaking. But did it give you a glimpse of God? Was your faith supported or challenged in any way? Would this conversation reflect your struggle to live out your Christian faith? Might God have a specific message for you that is coming through another person's words?

Journaling conversations from daily life may become an important spiritual discipline for you. You might also find it helpful to write conversations you wish you could have. Do you need to work through a conflict with your mother? Write your imagined sharing with her, and pray that such intimate understanding will occur in real life. Were there things you never had the chance to say to a friend now deceased? Use your journal to bring that relationship to completion.

Because conversations necessarily involve face-to-face encounters between human beings, you may find powerful emotions rising within you as you place the reality of words onto the pages of your journal. If you are dealing with particularly painful memories or experiences, you may want to be in touch with your pastor, a counselor, or a close friend who can help you maintain a positive look at whatever is causing hurt.

Journaling also gives the time and space to write out conversations with God. How would you dialogue with the Eternal One about suffering? Would it be helpful to imagine God responding to your prayer? What might the Almighty want to say to you at this point in your life?

And what about a conversation with yourself? Do you feel confused about a difficult decision? Are you unhappy with your life? Write a dialogue/conversation with yourself. Remember Tevya of *Fiddler on the Roof*? His life was often balanced out by dialogue with God and with himself. Tevya made sense of his experience of Jewish persecution by "talking it out" through inner and divine dialogue.

Journaling conversations, whether real or imagined, whether with ourselves or God, a friend or the Soviet president, can provide insight and understanding into our unique spiritual journey. Whereas in actual interaction with others we may feel limited by politeness or the need for privacy or concern for another's feelings, in our journal we are free to open ourselves honestly to the God who is present in every word we speak or hear.

This week, begin your journaling time as usual with some centering exercise to relax you into receptivity to God's power working in your life. Then spend your time either writing out the gist of an actual conversation or creating dialogue with another as you would like it or need it to happen. Don't worry about the form. Make simple designations of who is speaking when. Add editorial comments as needed, such as "his eyes blazed when he said this" or "her voice became lower and softer at this point" or "I had a hard time hearing this."

When you have finished writing, take whatever moments in prayer are appropriate to the conversation, relationship, or need. Be assured that your words (detailing of actual or imagined dialogue) are heard and understood by the God who loves you more than you will ever know. Know that just as daydreams can be lived into reality, so your words (even when written just for yourself) can lead to wholeness in Jesus Christ.

NOTES

1. Fynn, *Mister God, This Is Anna* (London: Collins, 1974), pp. 39-41

JOURNALING CONVERSATIONS OR DIALOGUES

Epilogue

Looking to the Future

For six weeks you have given yourself to the Christian discipline of journaling. You have tried a week of finding the meaning in your own life experience, and you have used scripture as the basis for journal-writing. Guided meditations have taken you to new worlds of imagination, and you have also been transported by your own dream adventures and stories. You have seen how your reading can be grist for the journal mill, and you have taken time to write down conversations and dialogues as a way of knowing God more intimately.

Undoubtedly, one or two methods have stood out as most interesting or practical for you personally. We hope you have found a combination of techniques that you can use as you continue to journal your spirit journey. You may have become aware that on a certain type of day you need the word of God enfolding you before journaling but that on another day you need to sit right down and begin a dialogue with God or your inner self. All these methods can be helpful and may be combined with other disciplines such as Bible study, retreats, fasting, and silence.

Just as each person is special and unique, so each approach to journaling will be intrinsically that person's own. Your journal should reflect who you are at a specific point in your life. The same journaler may use a flower-covered book with neat, tiny writing in blue ink for a time, yet later write in bold black printing in a brown spiral notebook. She may hold agonized conversations with God about world suffering and her own unhappiness. Pages later, she may sing God's praises for the wonder and beauty of life. Her journaling style will change as her life changes; the act of journaling reminds her, however, that God the Creator never changes. Journaling keeps her mindful that she is loved, treasured, and undergirded through all of life's changes.

There will be times in your life when it is helpful to review your journal. You might start a tradition of a once-a-year retreat when you read through the pages that detail so much of your life: feelings, questions, growth. This could be a time to take stock of your life in God. How is my faith growing? Which scripture verses continue to strengthen me? Other life-events will send you to the journal. How did I handle a similar problem? Have I written down memories of my good friend who is sick with cancer? Would the conversation with my spouse last Christmas help me understand how he is feeling now?

Your journal is for your eyes only (unless you choose to share parts of it with a trusted friend). Those with whom you live must understand how important it is that journal-writing be private. The assurance that this writing is for yourself alone will give you the confidence to write in total honesty and self-revelation. Some people even include a provision in their will that, upon their death, their journals are to be destroyed. Before you write such a stipulation, consider carefully these questions: Would my loved ones better understand me (in all my strengths and weaknesses) if they were to read my journal after I die? Would they be able to see me with the eyes of love and understanding, knowing the journal to be a gift of insight into who I really was? If you make such a legal provision, tell your friends and family of your wishes so that, if they sort through your possessions before the reading of a will, they will clearly understand the privacy that is so important to you.

However private you want to keep your journal, it is wise to include your name and address in the front of it in case you lose it. Losing a journal can feel like having a big chunk of your life taken away from you—as if you had lost precious photo albums in a fire. You want to have every chance of the journal's being returned to its rightful owner; no one else would care so deeply for these pages.

As you continue the Christian discipline of journaling, you will discover new, helpful methods that you can incorporate into your own personal journaling style. Here are some suggestions:

• Creative expression through artwork can enrich your journaling experience. You might use markers or watercolors to illustrate your journal entries. How could one paint joy? What colors might reflect your faith-questioning?

You might want to buy some clay and try sculpture. In response to Bible study, how might your hands fashion the face of Bartimaeus or the joy of the tenth leper who returned to give thanks to Jesus?

Just as grammar and penmanship are not of ultimate importance in your writing, so artistic skill (or lack of it) should not hold you back from incorporating any creative expression into your journaling. What you draw or sculpt is for you alone unless you choose to share it.

• You may feel called to write your autobiography. This could be done as a short three pages or as a long, detailed project. Either way, you would want to think through which aspects of your life illustrate how your faith has developed, how God has worked through your life, toward where your faith journey is taking you. You might want to choose old photographs to accompany your words. This could be the focus of a one- or two-day retreat: examining your life so far.

If you have unresolved griefs or anger or any other extremely negative emotion, you might want to surround yourself with as much love and support as possible during this writing process. A Christian counselor or retreat center staff person, minister, friends, or family might undergird you in prayer and presence as you undertake this project.

• Devotional books can be helpful companions to journaling the spiritual journey. The following books are practical guides to various aspects of one's spirit-journey:

Beginning to Pray by Anthony Bloom (Paulist Press, 1970). This Orthodox archbishop shares stories from his personal life to illustrate how prayer can come alive.

Every Bush Is Burning: A Spirituality for Today (Twenty-Third Publications, 1986) explores "the connection between ordinary reality and extraordinary grace, between everyday events and the divine mystery manifested in them."

Reaching Out: The Three Movements of the Spiritual Life by Henri Nouwen (Doubleday, 1975) describes the movements from loneliness to solitude, hostility to hospitality, and illusion to prayer.

Prayer for Pilgrims: A Book About Prayer for Ordinary People by Sheila Cassidy (Crossroad, 1982) tells of the "living dialogue which includes both talking to God and learning to be silent with him...the encounter with the risen Christ ...that touches every aspect of a person's life."

The River Within: The Search for God in Depth by Christopher Bryant (The Upper Room, 1983) looks at life stages and how each person, in the life journey, can "cooperate with God and grow to full human stature."

The Reed of God by Caryll Houselander (Arena Lettres, 1978) is a beautiful look at the Virgin Mary written devotionally in a way that helps us look at our own lives in Christ.

We Drink from Our Own Wells: The Spiritual Journey of a People by Gustavo Gutiérrez (Orbis, 1984) presents a Latin

American spirituality that arises out of the "theology of liberation."

Growing Strong at Broken Places by Paula Ripple (Ave Maria Press, 1986) looks at suffering—its source, effects on our lives, and how it can be transformed into a "guide leading us beyond ourselves."

Live the Questions Now: The Interior Life by Beth Rhude (Women's Division, Board of Global Ministries, The United Methodist Church, 1980) is a collection of stories, images, and exercises that form "a collage by women journeying toward communion with self, others, nature, and God."

Pilgrim at Tinker Creek; Teaching a Stone to Talk; Holy the Firm (Harper and Row, 1985, 1982, 1984) and other writings of Annie Dillard explore the mystic nature of the universe through incredibly beautiful prose.

The Potter and the Clay by Thomas Hawkins (The Upper Room, 1986) uses images of potter and clay to explore spiritual formation of the Christian.

Soul of My Soul: Reflections from a Life of Prayer by Catherine de Hueck Doherty (Ave Maria Press, 1985) is a sharing of one woman's intimate life with God. She writes, "Prayer is the meeting of two loves: the love of God and our love."

Prayer Is a Hunger by Edward Farrell (Dimension Books, 1972) is an easy-to-read exploration of many aspects of the spiritual life.

• Some books on the spirit journey include written exercises that help the reader/journaler focus on particular life issues, prayer concerns, theological development. Any of the following resources could be additionally used by an individual or group:

Right Here, Right Now: Spiritual Exercises for Busy Christians by Christopher Carstens and William P. Mahedy (Ballantine/Epiphany, 1985) presents a wide variety of spiritual exercises that can be included in an active life.

The Workbook of Living Prayer; The Workbook of Intercessory Prayer; The Workbook on Spiritual Disciplines by Maxie Dunnam

(The Upper Room, 1975, 1979, 1984) all offer a six- or seven-week study on a specific theme, with daily foci of reading, scripture, and journaling response.

A Thirty-Day Experiment in Prayer: Beginning a Prayer Journal by Robert Wood (The Upper Room, 1978) has daily scripture, prayer, and questions for reflection/action "for a month's journey into the habit of conversing with the Highest and Best."

Working Out Your Own Beliefs: A Guide for Doing Your Own Theology by Douglas E. Wingeier (Abingdon, 1980) uses scripture, tradition, experience, and reason in an easy-to-read guide to developing a personalized faith system. Each chapter has helpful exercises for journaling.

• Reading sermons or meditations on scripture can spark our own writing. Here is a sampling of books that might be helpful devotional material:

A Faithing Oak: Meditations from the Mountain by Robert A. Raines (Crossroad, 1982).

The Magnificent Defeat; The Hungering Dark and other books by Frederick Buechner (Seabury Press, both 1985).

Spinning a Sacred Yarn: Women Speak from the Pulpit (The Pilgrim Press, 1982).

Bread for the Wilderness—Wine for the Journey (Word Books, 1976), and *His Power in You* (Doubleday, 1978) by John Killinger.

The Finger of God by Allan Boesak (Orbis Books, 1982).

Women and the Word—Sermons edited by Helen Gray Crotwell (Fortress Press, 1978).

God, the Disturber by Alan Walker (Waco Books, 1973).

• Certain works of fiction are particularly thought-provoking; they can cause the readers to think about their own faith in new ways. These books are not to be read for plot but as a means to come closer to God. The following novels have been personally challenging to me as I have worked out my own theology:

The Last Temptation of Christ by Nikos Kazantzakis (Simon and Schuster, 1971) is an unusual telling of Jesus' story. The author says, "that part of Christ's nature which was profoundly human helps us understand him and love him and to pursue his Passion as though it were our own."

Silence by Shusaku Endo (Taplinger Publishing, 1979) "tells the story of a seventeenth century Portuguese priest in Japan at the height of the fearful persecution of the small Christian community." The novel helps the reader consider the difficulty of keeping faith when God appears to be absent and silent.

Barabbas by Par Lagerkvist (Vintage Books, 1951) is a novel by the Nobel Prize-winning author that tells the story of the man released when Jesus was sentenced to die. Lagerkvist imagines Barabbas to have been changed by the experience and influenced toward Christianity.

The Last Western by Thomas S. Klise (Argus, 1974) introduces us to Willie, "an innocent and a dreamer... who rises to prominence first as a baseball phenomenon, then as a religious leader and peacemaker" and ends up trying to save the world.

A Wrinkle in Time; A Wind in the Door; and *A Swiftly Tilting Planet* by Madeleine L'Engle (Dell Books, 1962, 1973, 1978) explore questions of good and evil through the believable adventures of Meg and Charles Wallace, a sister and brother who become involved in extraterrestrial travel and relationships.

Medicine Woman by Lynn V. Andrews (Harper and Row, 1981) tells of Native American culture and spirituality as the author is influenced by Agnes Whistling Elk, a shaman of incredible power.

The Book of the Dun Cow by Walter Wangerin, Jr. (Pocket Books, 1978) uses Chanticleer the Rooster and his world to explore questions of good, evil, and personal integrity in a glorious fantasy.

The Greek Passion by Nikos Kazantzakis (Simon and Schuster, 1971) "tells the story of a Greek village under Turkish domination and of how the lives of the villagers are changed—some to tragedy, some to self-fulfillment—by the roles they play in the annual drama of the Passion of Christ."

The Clowns of God by Morris West (William Morrow, 1981) uses the story of Pope Gregory XVII, a man of God who receives a vision that the world will end soon and, as he seeks to share the vision, discovers that the church and world are not ready to receive such news.

The City of Joy by Dominique Lapierre (Doubleday, 1985) tells of the poorest section of Calcutta and its inhabitants: "an epic story about the soul of humanity: a song of love, a hymn to life, a lesson in tenderness and hope for all people for all times."

As you continue in the practice of Christian journaling, you will find yourself more and more in tune with God in all of life. An evening at the theater or a movie, a new book of poetry, a telephone call from a good friend may trigger the need to journal. You will find the aspects of your own life that call you forth to pen and paper.

There may be certain periods in your life when journaling seems difficult. Perhaps you will find many excuses why *not* to journal: There just does not seem to be time. Journaling does not seem to mean as much as it used to. Be gentle with yourself during these times, but also look deeper to see if there is something blocking your writing that needs to be dealt with. Are you feeling depressed and unmotivated to journal? Journaling might be just what you need to begin the journey out of depression. Are you overextended? Maybe a half hour of journaling could help you refocus and prioritize your time. You do not feel the need to talk with God? Putting pen to paper might open up the lines of communication again.

It is unrealistic for most people to expect to write in their journal every day for the rest of their lives. But most of us can benefit immensely from journaling as a regular or even occasional discipline combined with other disciplines of the

Christian faith. Rabindranath Tagore writes of how our spiritual journeys come in the midst of a changing world. His poem is my prayer for you as you continue to journal *your* spirit journey:

> Before the end of my journey
> may I reach within myself
> the one which is the all,
> leaving the outer shell
> to float away with the drifting multitude
> upon the current of chance and change.[1]

NOTES

1. Rabindranath Tagore, *Fireflies* (New York: Macmillan, 1976), p. 272.

About the Author

Anne Broyles is a copastor of Malibu United Methodist Church in Malibu, California. Her ministry has included a position at Christ United Methodist Church in Norwalk, California and a cochaplaincy at the Wesley Foundation at the University of Michigan. Ms. Broyles is on the advisory board of *Weavings* and is active in Methodist Federation for Social Action.

Previous writings by the author have appeared in *Weavings*, *Journeying through the Days 1988*, *The Other Side*, and *Friends Journal*. This is her first book.

Ms. Broyles and her husband Larry Peacock are the parents of two children, Trinity Joy and Justus Simon. The family lived in the Quaker community of Pendle Hill for a year.